DISCARDED

THE MIRRORS OF 1932

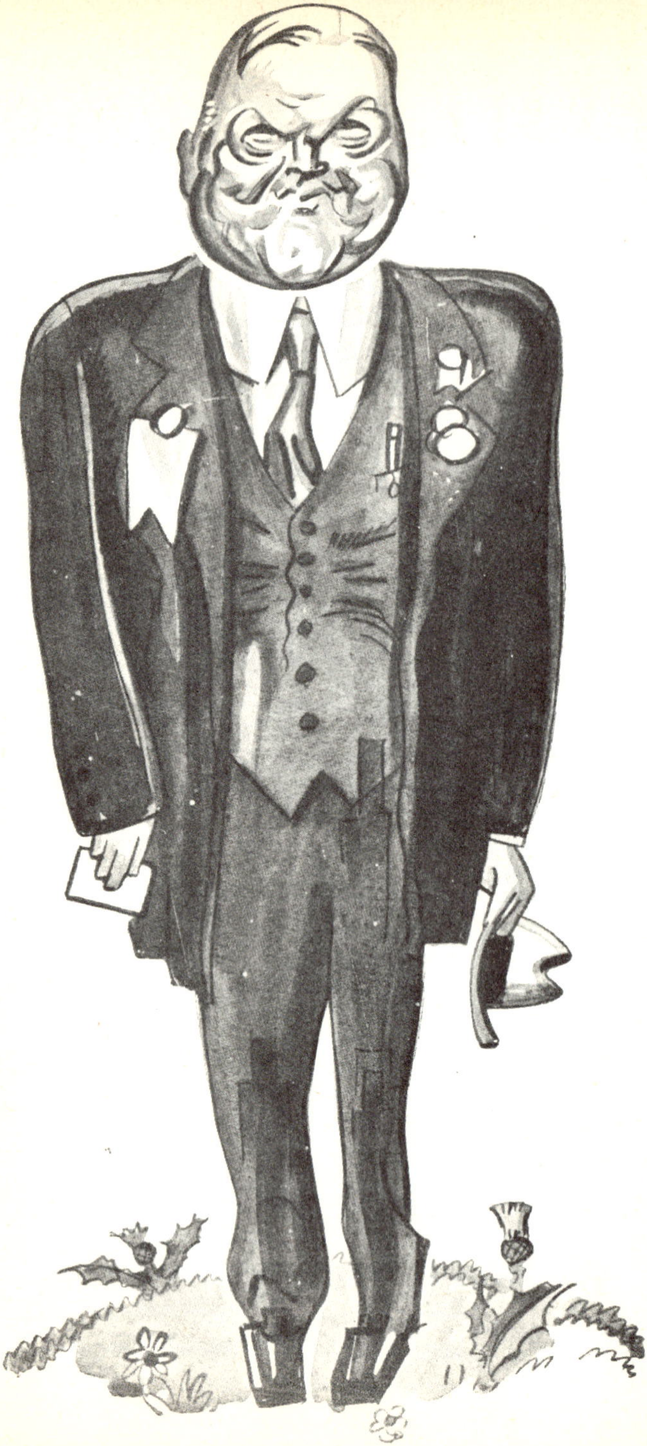

THE MIRRORS
OF
1932

RAY THOMAS TUCKER

With 10 Cartoons
by Cesare

Essay Index Reprint Series

BOOKS FOR LIBRARIES PRESS
FREEPORT, NEW YORK

First Published 1931
Reprinted 1970

INTERNATIONAL STANDARD BOOK NUMBER:
0-8369-1779-0

LIBRARY OF CONGRESS CATALOG CARD NUMBER:
78-121508

PRINTED IN THE UNITED STATES OF AMERICA

CONTENTS

Herbert Hoover	3
Alfred Emanuel Smith	33
Calvin Coolidge	55
Franklin D. Roosevelt	77
Dwight Whitney Morrow	101
Senator Joseph T. Robinson	127
Albert C. Ritchie	151
Owen D. Young	173
Newton D. Baker	195
Gifford Pinchot	213
John Barleycorn	233

HERBERT HOOVER

HERBERT HOOVER

It explains a great deal about Herbert Hoover to learn that he was not a "swimming hole kid."

An embittered Quaker orphan, silent, sullen, secretive, he had no playmates, and he suppressed the hunger for them. He collected rocks along the railroad tracks and fished along muddy Iowa ditches—alone. He was shunted from one grim and grubbing Quaker family to another, growing up in an atmosphere of religious restraint and social suppression, and he resented fiercely his poor boy state.

Worldly success—a "fortune," by his own admission—promised release, and he surrendered himself to its service. To this day he has not changed, he cannot if he would, and he is paying the price of drudgery and discipline. So is the American people.

Life, I think, has been unkind to Mr. Hoover. It gave him easy and excessive wealth too early. Had he mingled with the gang, and learned to fight, he might be a more effective figure. His lonely existence throughout his mining career accentuated his introversion, and in the White House he emerges as a sort of boarding school politician. Mr. Hoover, as was said of Charles Evans Hughes in 1916, "can hardly be classed as a member of the human family."

Though bewildered and depressed by fate's twistings, he refuses to recognize that those serviceable words—"efficiency" and "superman"—will die, politically, upon his departure from the White House. Mr. Hoover's mood, even in blackest moments, is that of an engineer who trusts himself to start the machine if his groping fingers can somehow come upon the proper lever.

His exceeding vanity, of course, prevents him from acknowledging any lack of mental or bodily warmth, or from striving to compensate for it. Likewise it keeps him from accepting the popular estimate of himself as President. He will not quit voluntarily; he will not see the sly hints that he refuse a renomination. He thinks that the breaks have been against him and that he deserves another chance.

He will undoubtedly get it. If he does, his campaign will differ little from that of 1928. He will make few addresses, and those will be generalities and platitudes. In appealing to Conservatives, he will let his reactionary record speak for him. To Progressives he will point out, as he did to our Porto Rican wards, that "economic independence" is the strongest bulwark of freedom and advancement. He will again urge them to swap their credos for the dim prospect of "two chickens in every pot and two cars in every garage."

He will be, again, all things to all men. He hopes to win, as he did before, through mistakes and meannesses in his opponents' camp. Meanwhile, his henchmen are already preparing to conduct another campaign based on sectional, religious and alcoholic prejudices.

I doubt if they can do it—again. For one thing, where will he get his newspaper support? The Scripps-Howard chain, which nominated him in 1928, will hardly be for him. William Randolph Hearst will probably break away, although I would not wager on it. The Chicago *Tribune* has urged that the party look "elsewhere" for a leader.

I understand that George Horace Lorimer of the *Saturday Evening Post* may drop him, or at least be indifferent. Southern and independent journals will not praise him, as they did when they knew him only as Hoover of Belgium and the Department of Commerce.

THE MIRRORS OF 1932

There is left the New York *Herald Tribune*. Wet and Wall Streetish, it will swallow hard, grumble a bit, mumble at his policies and then do as it always does—support the ticket. Numerous newspapers of that ilk will tag along, but half-heartedly. Few editors really like or admire Mr. Hoover. Their correspondents at the Capital like him less each day.

He is an unpopular and unloved man. Only his closest friends have any measure of his sense of loneliness and desperation.

For a decade he dreamed of the presidency, thus solacing himself for want of those political qualities—brass and ballyhoo—that might land him there. He knew, of a certainty, that he could run the nation better than either of his two superiors—Warren G. Harding and Calvin Coolidge—and he grinned innocently at their ineptitude and incompetence.

When "Bill" Vare and the remnant of the Ohio gang rushed him to victory over a coalition of Wall Street and the Old Guard, he deemed it to be destiny leaping in the Republican womb. When prejudice and passion made him President, he was content and confident.

HERBERT HOOVER

The Great Engineer and his Noble Experiments were to remake government and reform politics. He said as much. On the day after his nomination he expressed a low opinion of the financiers and politicians who had opposed him.

"I owe nothing to them," he told a friend, "and they know it."

There was then hope for Herbert Hoover.

Now he finds himself set down as a failure whom his orphaned party would cast aside, if practical politics permitted. Could there be keener cause for disappointment than that the Saviour of Belgium and the jack-of-all-trades of two Cabinets should be ranked by contemporary historians—the people and the politicians—with the Polks, the Pierces, the Buchanans, our third-rate Presidents!

He cannot comprehend. What a descent, he must reflect, for the world hero who was to reorganize us in accord with the best blueprints, and, simultaneously, furnish to the American people a demonstration of practical idealism in public affairs! It is only when we compute his deeds by his dreaming that his predicament, as it reacts upon himself, can be sensed in all its appalling consequences.

His idolators attribute deferment to circumstances beyond his control, such as Wall Street and Providence. These factors, however, may be allowed full weight without making out Mr. Hoover to be a man more sinned against—by that same Providence which elected him—than sinning. Nor is it sufficient to dismiss him, as does Senator "Jim" Watson of Indiana, by saying that he "knows less than a child about politics."

When he crossed the White House portico on March 4, 1929, he brought the elements of failure with him.

I confess that I did not discern them then. With many others I believed in the legend—wanted to believe. Even cynics conceded that Mr. Hoover would be an improvement upon his precedessor, who had, similarly, been an improvement upon Mr. Harding.

But he who runs may read the record.

Mr. Hoover lacks something more fundamental than political intelligence and an instinct for government. He is wanting in almost all the qualities which make for great, or even fair Presidents. He suffers from those which, except to one blessed with Mr. Coolidge's luck, lead to irreparable mistakes.

The presidency requires a directness of mind and a strength of character which Mr. Hoover has shown he does not possess. The White House needs a cooperative spirit, and he is a stark, selfish individualist, not in a sinister or philosophic sense, but in that he believes himself divinely right always. It requires a rough and resourceful, a Rooseveltian or Wilsonian personality, and Mr. Hoover is, by turn, fretful and feeble. He is a victim of self-pity; he is our first hairshirt hero.

No Chief Executive of modern times was so vacillating. Roosevelt rode into political storms, Taft bowed before them, Wilson broke, Harding bent, Coolidge put his fingers in his ears—but Mr. Hoover blows about.

It is only through the accident of his opportunism that he is now a Republican President. He might have been, in fact he came near to being a Democratic candidate for the office. In all his career there is no circumstance more illuminating than that by which Mr. Hoover, after serving under a Democratic Administration, became a Republican office-seeker.

In the last year of the Wilson Administration Mr. Hoover's closest friends were Franklin K. Lane, who was then Secretary of the Interior, and Franklin D. Roosevelt, who was Assistant Secretary of the Navy. The three families were wont to spend Sunday evenings together in a most informal manner. The men smoked and talked, while the wives went into the kitchen to stir up a cold Sabbath supper.

It was inevitable that the three men, so alike in many ways, should discuss the 1920 presidential prospects and Mr. Hoover's political affiliations. He himself had given no public sign. While the politicians and journalists speculated, he remained, as ever, a sphinx. He could not, it seemed, let them in on the great mystery of whether he was a Republican or a Democrat.

With Mr. Lane and Mr. Roosevelt he was more frank. It appeared that he had no deep political convictions. Whereupon, Mr. Lane proposed that he become a candidate for the Democratic presidential nomination. It was Mr. Lane's belief that Mr. Hoover could capture about fifty delegates for the 1920 convention, and although he might not win the nomination that year, he would be in an advantageous position for 1924.

Mr. Lane, a most persuasive person, convinced Mr. Hoover of the wisdom of this plan. The latter consented to announce himself as a Democrat when it seemed opportune.

There was nothing which the Republicans

dreaded more. They did not like Mr. Hoover, did not want him as their candidate, but they wanted him in their camp. So the late Henry Cabot Lodge and the late Boies Penrose set out to lassoo him. Although Mr. Lodge acted as emissary, Mr. Penrose was the gay deceiver. He gave a typical touch of reality to the comedy by pretending to denounce the whole thing, and he saw to it that Mr. Hoover got word of his opposition.

Mr. Hoover fell for it. The Senator from Massachusetts, smooth and smiling, persuaded Mr. Hoover that his best bet was to join the Republican Party. Mr. Lodge's logic convinced his victim that the Democrats had only a faint chance to carry the country either in 1920 or in 1924.

Meanwhile, speculation anent Mr. Hoover's plans continued. . . .

It was soon ended. Mr. Roosevelt and Mrs. Augustus Gardiner, the daughter of Senator Lodge, met at a dinner party in the spring of 1920. The two began to discuss politics.

"Mr. Hoover is to make a very interesting statement in a few days," said the daughter of the Senator.

"Yes," agreed the friend of Mr. Hoover, "so I understand. It ought to be very interesting."

"Yes," continued Mrs. Gardiner, "he is going to announce himself as a Republican."

"No," replied Mr. Roosevelt as he smiled into his soup, "he is going to announce himself as a Democrat."

"Oh, no!" protested Mrs. Gardiner, "he is going to announce himself as a Republican. Maybe I've said too much already, but he has promised my father that he would come out as a Republican."

She was correct. Although Mr. Hoover was entered in the early Michigan primary as a Democrat, and uttered no protest against this falsification of his position, his canvass showed him that Mr. Lodge was a wiser politician than Mr. Lane. Mr. Hoover became a Republican—at least in name.

For once, he was right. It led him to the presidency.

How unlike our great Presidents he has shown himself!

Our most constructive Presidents—Jefferson, Lincoln, Roosevelt—liked people. Mr. Hoover detests and dreads the mob; he mingles with only a few, and with them not for long. Though he is a Rotarian, he cannot be regular. His is a detailed, though somewhat disorderly, mind. He gives off light, not heat. He is as dynamic as a 30-watt bulb.

HERBERT HOOVER

His friends deny this analysis. But I am speaking of Hoover the President, not Hoover the Man. Although his presidential record tends to obscure his earlier achievements, I would not. Yet he himself described his service in Belgium as "the biggest wholesale grocery job in history," and he shook his head when that first troop of Hoover Boy Scouts—the Tom Gregorys, the Vernon Kelloggs and George Barr Bakers—dangled the presidency before him, if only by their own political palpitations.

Even the Great Engineer role vanishes under some scrutiny. Mr. Hoover, it appears, was a promoter rather than a mining expert. His salary was $5,000 for mining work, $95,000 as a financial adviser. Once, when confronted with the choice of selfless service to science in the U. S. Geological Survey or a "fortune" in private development, he took the advice of two professors at that pragmatic institution, Leland Stanford University.

"Promotion . . . in the employ of such financiers," they wrote, "may lead to as good a position as there is in mining engineering."

Without detracting from his mining and feeding feats, it cannot be ignored by the interpretive historian that in Belgium he had behind him the money and the sentiment of mankind. Did obstacles arise which even those forces could not move, he relied upon that doughty, determined Presbyterian, Woodrow Wilson.

There were then none to say him nay. Even the premiers and marshals of the belligerent powers were his yes-men, as his Cabinet is now—as it ever must be if it hopes to keep happiness and harmony in the presidential household.

It is as true now as it was then that he can work with underlings but not with equals.

Alas! He no longer deals in blueprints, financial reports, low-grade ores, calories, commercial statistics, boom markets. He must abide with men and women—122,000,000 of them—individually and in the mass. He must give and take, compromise and concede.

The President of the United States must be 90 per cent politician, 10 per cent executive.

Yet he cannot be comfortable with individuals, and he is suspicious of the mass. He no longer serves as a shining knight on the edge of Flanders Fields, or as a nation's salesman. He must stand on his own unheroic feet. He must keep his balance on a political reef washed by conflicting currents which he can neither cajole nor control.

HERBERT HOOVER

Through the windows of the White House we may glimpse—no more, for reasons to become apparent—the Herbert Hoover the Capital knows. It is as if, at last, an extraordinary specimen from foreign fields had been pinned to the laboratory table.

"He has an Oriental mind," said a grim Senator from a Far Western State. "He cannot act except by indirection preceded by a great deal of indecision."

A certain grizzly Senator from the Middle West phrases it more caustically. Once an admirer of the President, his forthright nature now inclines him to view Mr. Hoover, politically, as a "man without character or conviction." Euphemism, if naught else, inclines toward acceptance of the politer characterization. Within these classifications fall the salient weaknesses which Republicans on and off Capitol Hill discern in "the Chief."

There is, as illustration, his inability to look a person in the eye. Friendly biographers attribute this strange trait in so cosmopolitan a man to "shyness." They romance upon his habit of drawing circles and squares, head and eyes bent upon the point of his pencil, during an interview. It is, they say, the engineer's mind in motion—or in flight.

Maybe so. It is also a calculated means of escaping commitments. Those nods of his may be meant for assent, but the visitor cannot tell. In consequence, each caller quits the White House with the conviction that he has penetrated Mr. Hoover's consciousness. The latter, however, promises nothing. He hesitates and equivocates—by design, it seems. Throughout his career he has carefully refrained from accepting responsibility which he cannot disclaim should it prove expedient.

Between himself and those with whom he negotiates he interposes couriers, courtiers and second-hand interviewers. Thus he has for confidential secretary one Larry Richey, born Ricci, whose splendid training was acquired as a boy sleuth in the William J. Burns agency. His three other secretaries stand between himself and reality, responsibility.

In the great crises of his life, not excluding his maneuvering for the presidential nomination and election, he relies upon this indirect and irresponsible form of negotiation. There are few men and women—living—who can say: "Thus Herbert Hoover spoke to me and thus he said——".

His representatives in the Senate and House cannot wring a definite Aye or Nay from him even in the most critical struggles. They offer volumes of sage advice, but he listens not. If they urge immediate action, he does nothing. If they recommend delay, he moves frenziedly. In almost every instance he ignores their suggestions.

So many needless dilemmas does he create that they long since abandoned him to himself and his sycophantic counsellors. Cabinet and Secretariat through ignorance or a desire to please, tell him what he prefers to hear. They know that he cannot endure the truth if it be unpleasant.

Early in the administration Mr. Watson and Vice-President Curtis sought to guide his unsteady steps. But bitter memories bothered Mr. Hoover. Had not the Senator branded him as a "Britisher" at Kansas City! Had not the Vice-President opposed his nomination on the theory that it must be accompanied by an "apology to the American people"!

Therefore, their sincerity was suspect. Toward them he has ever been suspicious and sensitive. Even "Charley" McNary, who grew up with Mr. Hoover in Oregon and attended Leland Stanford with him, is not trusted, simply because he belongs to that strange variety of men known as politicians. Now these hard-boiled advisers go near him only when commandeered and carried to the White House in the Presidential limousine.

"Jim" begged him not to assail the Senate's relief program as "playing politics at the expense of human misery." The Hoosier statesman, therefore, was horrified to learn that the President contemplated another tirade against a Senate, which on paper at least, was controlled by his own party.

"Yeah," groaned the Senate leader, "I suppose he will. He's just like a little baby. He has found he can wriggle his toes, he did it once, he liked it and he'll do it again."

Mr. Hoover, perhaps rightly, thinks all politicians to be inherently selfish and insincere, and not to be trusted. He has imbued his Cabinet with the same suspicion. Let a candidate for the judiciary present the endorsement of the Republican organization of his State, and Attorney General Mitchell is apt straightway to conclude that he must be a shyster.

Did Mr. Hoover possess the courage of his convictions with respect to the general worthlessness of politically minded men, and battle them toe-to-toe in Rooseveltian manner, he would have their confidence and admiration, even though it were tinged with hostility. As it is, he has neither; they simply tolerate him. Toleration by his party and truckling by his friends form a disastrous combination for even the most splendidly equipped President.

As with Congress, the White House has been a gloomy place since Mr. Hoover moved in. Main Street it may have been during the Harding habitation, and the Old Homestead when Calvin Coolidge dozed there, but it has been transformed into a three-shift factory. It reflects the man who sits inside as do his unvarying double-breasted blue suits and stiff collars.

His routine is the shortest distance between two points—his bedroom and his office. From 8.30 to 6.30 Mr. Hoover confers and interviews and dictates, until one wonders when he thinks. He has, indeed, time only for a scant nod to the Secret Service men who guard him, for the attachés who run his errands, for the clerks who pile his desk with papers.

The White House is no longer one of the "better homes" such as Mr. Hoover's conference would erect in rows across the land, along with the "abolition" of the poor house. It is a grim and efficient center where the Great Engineer labors, ten hours each day, and often after hours, to come upon the lever that will start the machine.

Mr. Hoover has not yet learned to frolic. There

is a period of exercise each morning, and it is called, appropriately enough, "the medicine ball game." In reality it is a heavy-handed half-hour of agony for those who must attend. Cabinet members, Associate Justices and Secretaries toss a heavy ball around amid grunts and groans and black eyes sustained in a daredevil fling. Fifteen minutes elapse. Then the carelessly clad group climb creakingly into their cars and drive away.

Yet it is the only exercise the President takes. He does not golf, walk, ride, swim, attend the theater, go to the movies or indulge in light reading. For recreation he still fishes. For mental distraction he reads detective stories, but as an engineer rather than a dilettante; he tries to outguess the author.

Insomnia afflicts him, and from midnight until four he is invariably awake. For these hours he stores up tomes of no particular merit and without method. His reading is wholly disorganized. One week he devours all discoverable data on Egyptian pyramids, and the next he studies the history of a forgotten tribe of African head-hunters.

Spiritual and physical loneliness bow him down. The Hoovers, in the White House and for many years in the past, call in guests for every meal.

These periods may be no more than vast and vacant silences. Unless Mr. Hoover chooses to talk, he consumes his food with eyes on his plate. He is a fast and voracious eater. He can be, if he cares to rouse himself, a charming monologist and autocrat of the table.

He summons people to sit up with him, and then, too, he can be quite a raconteur. Always, however, he seems to be fleeing from himself. In the midst of—for him—a racy discussion he lapses into a somber, and then, into a seemingly sullen and stubborn state.

Except to those who share his enjoyment of the silences of the brooks and fishes, week-ends at the camp on the Rapidan are a dull duty. Even the sport of casting is, to Mr. Hoover, only an escape from the sounds and contacts of civilization.

"It is a piscatorial crime," he once said, "to talk along a trout stream. The best friend then is a silent one."

Yet Mr. Hoover has many warm friends. They see in him something which binds them to him loyally and unselfishly. He is idolized by the men and women who worked with him in Belgium, in the Food Relief Administration, in the Department of Commerce. Though they concede his failure as a

President, it serves only to strengthen their sympathies. It affects them not.

I find few, however, who can define their feeling for him. It is, I imagine, the pathetic, wistful, helpless streak in his nature that appeals to them. They sense his unexpressed need for friendship. There is more of the parental than the pal in their almost impersonal affection. Though friendly biographers have made him the hero of many bright volumes, they cannot humanize him or kindle in other minds the spark of his personality which they cup so conscientiously.

It takes a friend to understand Mr. Hoover, and to realize that he is the natural progeny of his background and birthright. The Hoovers never sunk deep roots anywhere. His ancestors were ever changing their names, their dwelling places, their manners, their religions, since the first Hoefer was driven from France to Holland by a Catholic king in the fifteenth century.

Likewise, the President has spent his days as an Ishmaelite. The Sierras, Australia, the Orient, Russia, Burma, London knew him better than did his fireside, his political club, his meeting house. Small wonder that he should be, at heart, a vagrant, wanderlusting spirit, with no spiritual cultural, political depth.

It is an illuminating sidelight on Mr. Hoover that, when he first sought the presidency, his was an open door to public, press, politicians. Now he is more difficult to get at than King Tut. It is also significant that in those brave pre-convention days almost all the young and idealistic members of the Washington corps of correspondents were his valiants. Hardly a handful have faith in him now.

Better than anyone else they perceive these frailties of which I write. They, I know, have lost their admiration for his fine intelligence and high idealism. His speeches, his statements, his proclamations, in spirit but more often in style, are meaningless even to these trained dissemblers. Again and again, before telephoning or despatching advance releases to their offices, they must first trouble the Literary Secretary for an explanation—or at least for punctuation.

The President's "hairshirt letter" is an excellent example of his English, no more precise or pure now than when he flunked this course at Leland Stanford University and was enabled to graduate by a ruse. Were it not that Mr. Hoover has never

THE MIRRORS OF 1932

deemed it worth while to read a poem or drama, I would conclude from his literary style that he were a blind devotee of Robert Browning's youthful obscurities.

The public may think this a strained or supposititious characterization of our President, who occupies an office which we all revere. On the contrary, a study of Mr. Hoover's career reveals that nothing less—or more—was to be expected. The thread draws clear and true. From his boyhood in Iowa to his beleaguerment in the White House there is no break.

All these traits were limned in the 1928 campaign, but they were then charged to the exigencies of practical politics. Gabriel himself must have recognized that, in such an angelic creature as Mr. Hoover's friends said he was, the end justified the means.

For consider: Mr. Hoover alone of 122,000,000 people was unaware of the religious passions which his campaign was stirring, even though resentful and shamed Republicans deluged his Massachusetts Avenue headquarters with protests against the Willebrandting. From a desk outside the Candidate's door "Jimmie" Burke, the Pittsburgh barrister and boulevardier, revised Mabel's speeches so that they would be more understandable to the Bible Belters.

To the President's credit he seems slightly remorseful at the realization that he was elected upon such an appeal to prejudice.

Mr. Hoover does not like to recall those unhappy days when idealism was subordinated to booze and bigotry. It is not, perhaps, as the victims charge, ingratitude that induced him to banish his campaign advisers from his circle. It is rather an engineer's conviction that, once a machine has performed its function, it should be scrapped. Thus he has rid himself of Mrs. Willebrandt, "Wild Bill" Donovan, "Doc" Work, Horace Mann. Too many ghosts, he undoubtedly mused, as he found means for disposing of them.

Mabel he sent packing when he denied her a prized federal judgeship. He shattered young Donovan's Irish heart and faith when he would not name his Catholic friend to be Attorney General, and then sought to deport him to the Philippines as Governor General.

Mr. Hoover was quite impartial in withholding rewards, however. He has never thanked William E. Borah or Smith Wildman Brookhart for persuading the western farmers that he wore a halo rather than horns. It is true that he offered the post of Secretary of State to Mr. Borah, but it was grudgingly tendered and gleefully declined.

"He knew," growled the individualist from Idaho, "that I could not accept it, and thereby agree to approve in advance every act of his Administration."

The Hoover of the glorious days in Belgium underwent a metamorphosis during the campaign. Ambition's approach to a ten-year-old objective may be sufficient explanation. He promised a Wickersham investigation of prohibition solely as a form of strategy that would carry both New York and Texas, even though he does not believe in changing morals and manners by legislative decree. He permitted Mr. Borah and Mr. Brookhart to think, and so inform the farmer, that he would favor radical reform for the benefit of agriculture. His couriers and courtiers sped through the land scattering promises like grass seed.

His address in Madison Square Garden denouncing "state socialism" marked the disappearance of the old and other Hoover, if there was ever such a person. It antagonized and disillusioned every thoughtful liberal who had entertained hope of him. Miss Julia Lathrop, the famous social worker, immediately cancelled all the speeches she had scheduled on his behalf.

HERBERT HOOVER

It brought Senator Borah hot-foot from yellow fields of corn to the citadel of inner strength and righteousness on Massachusetts Avenue. In this crisis Mr. Hoover was as helpless as the political child he is. Susceptible to panicky fits when reverses threaten, he was "glassy-eyed," as one Senator describes his state on such occasions. He flopped his arms helplessly at his side, palms outward. So he placed himself in the strong hands of the Senator from Idaho.

There were days and nights of statements, squirmings and denials. There were councils of war and peace and cries of prosperity. But Mr. Borah eventually emerged with the promise of a special session of Congress for enactment of legislation exclusively designed to aid agriculture. Borah as a Hoover champion was the fair-haired boy.

But their friendship cooled when the President issued his call for the special session born of Mr. Borah's persuasion. Over the Senator's protests the President asked for tariff revision on behalf of industry as well as agriculture. He ignored the Idahoan's prediction that this would mean a selfish scrambling for industrial increases, and harm to the farmer.

Mr. Hoover had, as he always does, hearkened to other counsellors from the East, and there his heart lay. Sadly the Senator trudged back to Capitol Hill with another cross to bear and berate.

There have been other clashes and other pledges unkept, until the two no longer share the ecstasy of their earlier courtship. Mr. Borah assiduously assails Mr. Hoover's policies, and Mr. Hoover appoints Mr. Borah's enemies to office in Idaho.

If there were some who were not similarly fooled, it is because of previous experiences with the promising President. George Norris of Nebraska resisted all blandishments with a cynical smile. He recalled that time when the Republican candidate, through an emissary, as always, collaborated with him in framing the first post-war farm bill. It was to have been the Norris-Hoover solution of the agricultural problem.

But Mr. Hoover, twelve hours before he was scheduled to urge its adoption by a Senate committee, informed the Senator from Nebraska that he must speak in opposition. Mr. Hoover had learned that Calvin Coolidge was agin' the whole program, and, as a good Cabinet member, he heeded the voice from Vermont.

Even so, Mr. Hoover wanted the Nebraska radical as his running mate. Incredible as it may seem, the foe of "State socialism" implored the chief advocate of government operation of public utilities to team up with him in 1928. As Mr. Hoover's nomination became more certain, he grew panicky lest the West revolt.

His sensitive nature would not permit him, at first, to dwell on the prospect of political association with the senatorial candidates who had been questioning his citizenship, his Americanism, his Republicanism. So he hit upon Mr. Norris. To Senator Borah, Mr. Hoover's marshal at Kansas City, went a message requesting him to line up delegates for the Hoover-Norris ticket.

The Nebraska maverick denounced the fantastic proposal as soon as it was broached to him. But he recalls the incident ironically as he reflects upon the schemes to which Mr. Hoover permits his picked politicians to stoop in their efforts to drive the Senator from public life. In Norris's mind, at least, it stirs some suspicion of the depth of the President's philosophy and his professed attachment to the party's historic principles.

The sour Hiram Johnson also knew Mr. Hoover of old. Neither forgetting nor forgiving, "Hi" retains a clear recollection of Mr. Hoover's treatment of the late Senator James D. Phelan of California. He recalls that Senator Phelan, taking a liking to young Hoover many years ago, frequently befriended him at the Capital. "Jim" Reed's biting criticism of "this British interloper" never failed to bring Phelan to his feet in defense of Food Administrator Hoover. The Senator was patron and protector to the younger Californian.

By 1920, however, the Food Administrator had got presidential ambitions and Republicanism. As a test of his new-found faith, the G. O. P. leaders demanded that he indorse Samuel Shortridge as a Republican candidate against Mr. Phelan. It mattered not, Hiram remembers, that Senator Phelan was an old man, and Mr. Hoover's friend. Only three days before the election the appeal went out, and Mr. Phelan with it. It broke the ageing statesman's heart—according to Hiram—but it pushed Mr. Hoover toward the presidency.

Senator Phelan, like the Works, the Willebrandts, the Donovans, the Hustons, was merely a used and outworn machine. . . . In industry they call it obsolescence.

Had Mr. Hoover appreciated then or did he realize now, that men are not machines, and that statistics are no substitute for statesmanship, he would be a happier and greater man.

He would be assured, at the least, of a footnote in history.

ALFRED EMANUEL SMITH

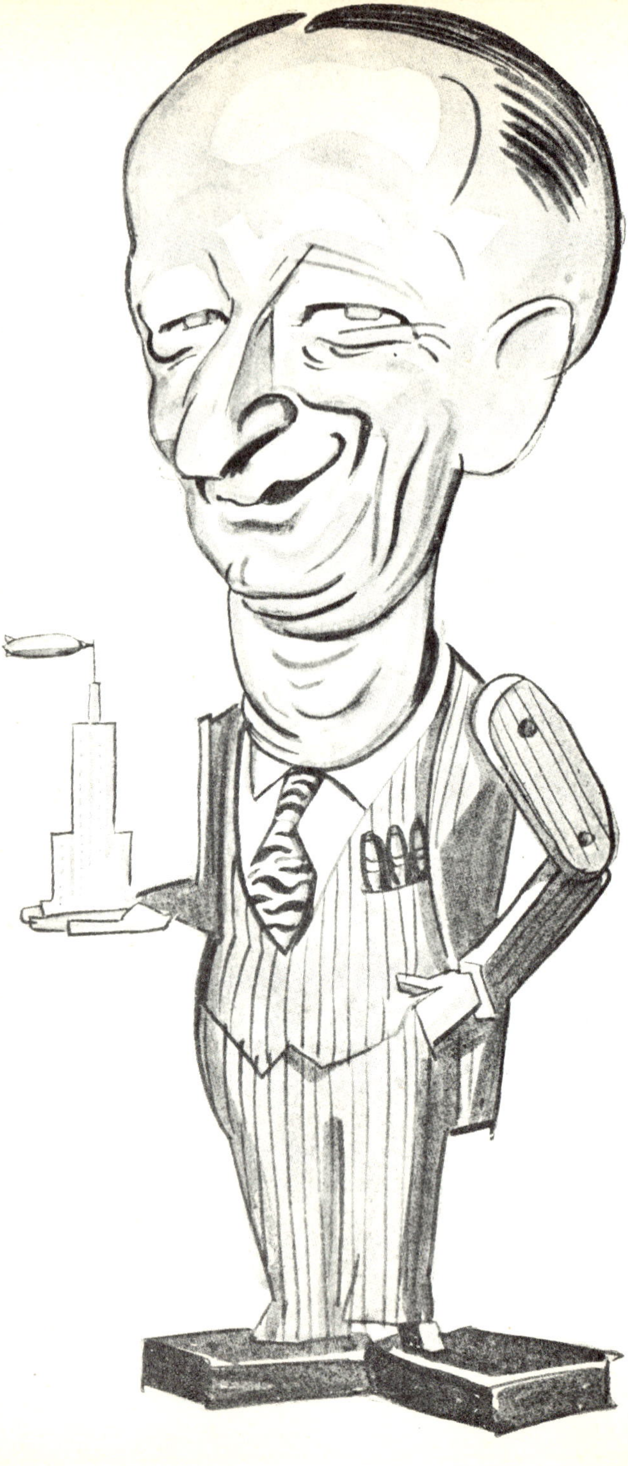

ALFRED EMANUEL SMITH

High life has spoiled that grinning, good-natured child of the tenements and the sidewalks of New York—Al Smith.

The story of his latter days may be told in a parable.

His wealthy associates, including National Chairman John J. Raskob, took him to the top of America's most lofty and dazzling structure, the Empire State Building, and bade him look down. All he saw would be his if he would but entrust himself to their hands, they whispered, and they threw in the presidency of the construction corporation.

And he looked, not toward Brooklyn Bridge where stands the humble home whence he sprang to become the most attractive actor on the modern political stage, but toward Park and Fifth Avenues and the dwelling places of ease and elegance he long had envied. And whatever angels hover above the Democratic Party recorded "one lost soul more."

THE MIRRORS OF 1932

He is no longer the grinning, gallant, gorgeous knight of the brown derby and cocked cigar over whom so many millions wept and smiled and cheered and thrilled only a short while ago.

The "barefoot boy of the Biltmore Hotel," as an ironic rival once dubbed him, has gone high-hat, high-brow and high-life.

The old, human, liberal impulses no longer stir him.

The former advocate of political reform has grown fat, physically and intellectually.

The waist line of his trousers and the head line of his derbies have had to be enlarged.

He now urges repeal of the direct primary. He scoffs at talk of power as a dominant issue in the 1932 campaign. He indorses Mr. Raskob's politically hermaphroditic program. To the millions who ask food he would give a drink.

He has become blind to the realities he once discerned so clearly and expounded so captivatingly.

Withal, he will not relinquish his nominal leadership of a party vainly striving—but still striving—to meet its responsibility as a liberal opposition to the reactionary Hoover Administration.

Al is, in short, the dog in the Democratic manger.

He endures enforced obscurity with poorer grace

ALFRED EMANUEL SMITH

than he stood prosperity when he had it. He cannot abide the loss of headlines and popularity. Demonstrations are a drug to him, the limelight as strong a stimulant as wine.

For he has the heart of a prima donna. He is the most theatrical figure in American politics.

He wants a second nomination, although he dare not—cannot—make an overt move to get it. He will not stand aside, unless circumstances command, even for his political protégé Governor Franklin D. Roosevelt of New York.

He is the victim of frustration—a sore and sour hero.

He is, too, a political giant whose limbs are pinned down by petty and parochial men—a Gulliver. He is loved by millions who cannot marshal their affection into political channels, but he is distrusted and disliked by a few leaders who, for the moment, hold his fate in their scheming hands.

Tammany hates him. So does Mayor James J. Walker of New York City. Ditto John Francis Curry, the boss of Tammany Hall. The district leaders and ward heelers of Gotham recall him, when they think of him at all, with resentment. There is none in his old kingdom to do him honor or obeisance.

THE MIRRORS OF 1932

Governor Roosevelt long since turned to other counsellors, dismissing the kitchen cabinet which his predecessor had created. Himself a candidate for the presidency, Mr. Roosevelt thinks that Mr. Smith should forego whatever ambitions he may still entertain. Moreover, the New York Governor, despite seeming differences, is on the best of terms with Tammany Hall.

It is these enemies of Al who will determine the New York Democrats' course and candidate. They will select the delegates to the national convention. Should they so decree, they may not include their former idol in the list of honorables. They may again rebuke him, as they did when they prevented him from attending the State convention in 1930 as a delegate.

It is entirely within the power of this coterie to push Al on or off the stage he treads so spectacularly but, to their mind, so selfishly.

Al is a dethroned monarch. The only trappings of royalty he has been permitted to take into exile are his brown derby, his cigar, his memories and his unfortunate East Side accent.

Yet he has, as he dwells on happier days, only himself to chide.

When he was boss, he insisted that the Tammany

troupe remain in the wings. It was his show, and a one-man act; he ran it accordingly. He dreaded lest his lowbrow supporters' antics might spoil his performance. He selected his appointees and advisers from among the foes of the regular organization—goo-goos, business men, trained experts, welfare workers.

He committed numerous other blunders. He attended Rockefeller weddings—in full dress, too—and Vanderbilt tea parties. He deserted Cherry Street for the Biltmore Hotel, later migrating to fashionable Park Avenue. He got, in the parlance of the gang, "a swelled head."

The presidency—for himself—then seemed at stake, and he governed with an honest and heavy hand. Tammany, he served notice, must undergo reform—a movement more apparent than actual. The box-office pickings for the boys were lean during his rule, and he was held responsible. He had violated the code of the spoilsmen.

Those were the days when we heard so much of the New Tammany, and Mr. Smith as its prophet.

He even essayed to lecture "Jimmie" Walker concerning the latter's regime and responsibilities as Mayor. The reply was premonitory.

"Listen, Al," retorted Broadway's Beau Brummel, "you're the Governor and I'm the Mayor. You run the State and I'll run the City."

Years ago Mr. Smith declined to appoint Mr. Curry as State Insurance Commissioner. The latter, apparently, did not fit into the scheme of the New Tammany. Now that Mr. Curry sits at the top through the turn of the political whirligig, he takes typical Tammany revenge. The two barely speak.

Mr. Smith, it seems, thought that he ought to function as honorary Governor even after the election of Mr. Roosevelt to that office. But the latter has bigger and better ideas. He wants to be Governor—and, perchance, President.

So their romantic friendship and their Alphonse-and-Gaston exchanges at Democratic national conventions during the last decade now appear to have been only so much political hokum. Their act fooled everybody but themselves.

Al has broken with the past—and the politicians.

The South and West still regard him as the Pope's political legate. They will not have him, as they showed in 1928.

Nevertheless, through his influence over "his little boy"—Mr. Raskob—he maintains a grip on the party machinery and the money bags. He must be reckoned with to the end of the 1932 campaign. He may be down but he is not out. More important still, the big interests like him, and always have.

He is a pathetic, but not yet a tragic figure.

No more tragic—or pathetic—than he was at Omaha that opening night of the 1928 campaign. There he exhibited a lack of understanding of himself and the American people—indeed, of practical politics—which may keep him from the White House even should his religion not prove sufficient bar.

It was an amazing, though an unconscious revelation, of the man who, until that moment, had acquired a reputation as the smartest politician and most astute student of popular psychology of his time.

Al was eating dinner preparatory to making his first address in a nationwide tour. It was the great moment toward which his thoughts had been directed for a decade. He—a Roman and an untutored lad born of humble, Irish parentage on the lower East Side—was to climax his romance with a chance at the White House.

As he toyed with his food, obviously impressed and oppressed, a member of his party approached and asked:

"How are you feeling, Guv'nor?"

Al could scarcely mumble a rejoinder.

"I'm scared, Charlie," he replied. "I'm wondering how it will go. I don't know these people out here. I don't speak their language. And I'm sort of scared."

The veteran of a score of fierce New York battles was shaking from stage fright. He brightened a bit at the cocky assurance that he would "knock 'em dead." At the next remark, however, he flushed.

"Now, Guv'nor," continued his voluntary adviser, "you're in a national campaign. You're not back in New York. Cut out the 'ain'ts' and 'raddios' and 'don'ts' for 'doesn'ts.' You can speak English with the best of them when you want to. Do it."

Al reddened, and was about to resent this frank suggestion. Then he recognized that it was well-meant, and he replied, slowly and thoughtfully:

"No, Charlie—you're all wrong. I'm goin' to campaign just as I am. I won't change now even to get in the White House. I'm goin' to run just as God made me."

So he did.

It was, without a doubt, the most starkly honest

ALFRED EMANUEL SMITH

moment of a presidential contest for which some Americans already feel shame. It was, perhaps, evidence of Mr. Smith's honesty and simplicity of spirit. But it also disclosed a fatal weakness which marred his conduct and his campaign, as it had his public career ever since he emerged from the ranks.

God—with apologies to Mr. Smith—did not make the man who set out to seek the presidency so chivalrously but so mistakenly that night in Omaha. Al himself had permitted his associations and his environment to perform that job. Indeed, he had not supervised an important part of it, or shown any solicitude for what the product might be.

There was a Carlylean carelessness in his growth.

In the years when he was growing and broadening in every other respect—mastering the intricacies of government, gaining a deep knowledge of men and women, leaving an imprint upon the character of a great State, winning the admiration and affection of high and low—he was, ironically, neglecting certain personal and political requisites.

He was neglecting those trivialities which we hold so essential when we choose our Presidents—idioms, idiosyncrasies, dress, manners and etiquette. He was dropping, and never reclaiming, his "g's," and he was confusing singular nouns with plural verbs. He was disregarding the constitutional right of every moron to pronounce r-a-d-i-o as it is spelled.

Only Al knows why. It seems, however, that he deliberately eschewed correct speech and conventional manners.

For years his mimicry of what he held to be affectations of speech and manners had convulsed his hero-worshippers at Albany. Even during the campaign he satirized his opponent's precise platitudes with a scornful pronunciation of the name of "Hoo-vah."

His nomination for the presidency did not—could not—change him. So he ran, he said, "as God made him." Never was a man more mistaken, or more in need of advice.

All his vast knowledge of government availed not against his bad grammar.

He overestimated the independence and intelligence of the electorate. He underestimated their sensitiveness as well as their powers of perception and prattling.

His speech cast a shadow over his campaign. His East Side accent provoked more discussion than his views on men and measures, his golden dentistry

ALFRED EMANUEL SMITH

more excitement than his prophetic denunciation of Republican prosperity.

The country could not see the statesman for the showman.

He marvelled at the millions who came to greet him. He did not sense that to these stay-at-homes he simply symbolized the coming of Manhattan to Mahomet. They turned out to stare but not to vote for him.

His gay get-up they contrasted—to his disadvantage—with Mr. Hoover's stiff, white collars and modeless, blue suits, his breezy bonhomeries with Mr. Hoover's conventional characteristics and stodginess of speech.

Al is too human and not enough of a humanist.

Had he had time for ever so little poetry or philosophy—or even Father McGuffey's Reader—he might have cultivated those accents and artificialities which we require in our Chief Executives.

He—not God—has failed in those superficial things which shape our statesmen and our history.

It avails not that he has most of the qualifications for the presidency, whereas Mr. Hoover lacks them. He has none of the qualifications for getting elected to that office.

THE MIRRORS OF 1932

For all his lore in the science of government, he is a political ignoramus.

He does not know that the American people prefer a stuffed shirt on the stump, and then complain when they discover that there is more stuffing than shirt to their chosen candidate.

Al's limitations showed more strikingly as the campaign progressed. He made no effort to conceal them. When correspondents sought his views on reparations, international debts, the League of Nations, he naïvely admitted that he was not equipped to comment. He got his information anent national and international affairs on the instalment plan from Representative "Joe" Byrnes and Norman H. Davis, and there was missing the fine familiarity of his State speeches.

He talked policies and personalities before strangers with a frankness rarely heard in politics. With boyish bravado he related secrets and intimacies he might better have withheld. He pleaded ignorance of national history and even geography, delivering an address on Boulder Dam at Denver under the misapprehension that it was a local problem.

In visiting parks and State Capitol halls, he admitted that it meant nothing to him whether Main

Street patriots had been hewn into marble by Houdon or Phidias.

He knows Broadway but not Main Street—the Bright Light but not the Golden Age or Bible Belt.

He would make no concessions to the sensitiveness of the simple folk who live west of the Hudson River—or west of the water towers. He refused to doff his brown derby. He wore his gayest and most striped suits. He climbed into the rigging of his automobiles and waved at skyscraper windows with the abandon of a performer in a circus cavalcade.

It was a great show, even a refreshing one—but hardly a proper pilgrimage toward the White House by a man already carrying so many handicaps of creed, background and nationality.

Behind these bright scenes, however, things were not going so well. Al soon discovered that running for office in New York and in the nation were two different undertakings. He found himself unable to stir a mass of 120,000,000 people as he had the 11,000,000 cosmopolites of his home State. He met an inertia—and a prejudice—which appalled him.

Yet he persisted with brave but futile courage.

Always he was waiting for the break that had

never failed him in his local contests. Always in the past young opponents had afforded him an opportunity to strike back devastatingly. An arch-opportunist and skillful campaigner, Al was confident almost to Election Day that sooner or later he would demolish an unwary and inexperienced Herbert Hoover.

There would be, Al told himself, a dropping of the Republican candidate's guard, and he would hit with the speed and strength of the master-politician.

He would win through a quip or a ruse or repartee. These were to be his weapons.

It was thus that he had transformed probable defeat into a triumph in 1924. When his gubernatorial rival, Theodore Roosevelt, capped a foolish and inaccurate statement by asking "Who told me that?" of his advisers, Al romped to the wire merrily. He convulsed the State with his mimicry of the unfortunate remark by "the little colonel"—his own description of his illustrious opponent—and conveyed the impression that Teddy had only second-hand knowledge of public affairs.

Similarly he had trounced Ogden L. Mills two years later. The latter, in an unguarded moment, declared that "there is no truth in the man (Smith) in public or private life." Although Mr. Mills simply meant to suggest that Mr. Smith was a political prevaricator—no serious charge—the latter seized upon the "private life" reference.

It was the moment for which Al had prayed. That night he delivered his now-famous "Great White Throne" sermon. He told in eloquent tones of his own marital faithfulness, and he challenged Mr. Mills—a divorced man—to do the same.

Mr. Smith, as always, gave a great show. His voice quavered, his eyes flashed, his face crimsoned, his hands trembled. His passion shook him visibly and it moved sympathetic hearers to even deeper emotion. Tears and groans and sobbing showed how deeply.

It was a dramatic and crashing climax—an excellent piece of political theatrics. It almost seemed as if it had been rehearsed earlier in the day. Under the spell of Al's artistry his audience forgot that the two men's experiences in wedlock was hardly a public issue. So did Al—perhaps.

It was by these same wiles that Mr. Smith, almost to the end, expected to defeat Mr. Hoover. Such a conception of a presidential campaign was, mayhap, to be expected of a man trained in the stirring school of New York politics, but it reflected a sorry misapprehension of national forces and sentiment.

Al, in all seriousness, hoped to win the White House as a thespian wins an ovation in the theater. He hoped to achieve the presidency as a performer captures applause. The political curtain was to ring down as he danced, gaily and grinningly, across the portico of the presidential mansion.

Mr. Hoover, however, gave no chance for a *coup de grace*. He held out neither his chin nor any political creed—only a few ambiguous generalities. He utilized the tactics of a groundhog. That was his idea of how the greatest office in the people's gift should be won.

So—issues and personal conflict wanting—they raised against Al his religion. They attributed a mediæval conception of Catholicism to a man whose understanding of other-world mysteries is as literal as any illiterate kleagle's.

The same issues—or prejudices—would dominate if Al runs again. He has not changed.

He is still the same clever and captivating fellow. He still radiates an irresistible charm that is poignantly mingled with personal and parochial crassness. He possesses the same gift for attracting the masses to him, the same genius for public affairs.

ALFRED EMANUEL SMITH

But he could not win—not even against Herbert Hoover.

His close relationship with Mr. Raskob would hurt him. The automobile magnate's smug attitude toward politics and government is not that which inspired Mr. Smith in happier days. Although an economic conservative always, his liberalism manifesting itself, like Charles Evans Hughes', in political reform, Mr. Smith, until lately, had more faith in the common people than his National Chairman shows.

In his loyalty to the Raskobian philosophy, Al exhibits some disloyalty toward his own record.

But he has ever been strangely susceptible to environment and associates, and loyal to those who have helped him. It is a trait of his race. Moreover, in Tammany Hall the cardinal sin is ingratitude—a charge which constitutes the pending indictment against Mr. Smith in the Wigwam. There they believe that he owes all his advancement to the organization, and that he should have no other idols.

Tammany conveniently passes over Al's record in this respect. It forgets that he entered politics as a foe of the organization out of simple gratitude to a ward boss who had befriended him. But when he was taken into "the Hall" by the late Charles F. Murphy, the latter had no more faithful vassal. For fifteen years Al had no ideas and no ideals other than those which Mr. Murphy entrusted to him.

He was just another Tammany man—no better and no worse than the next.

As Assembly leader at Albany he performed the boss's errands without question, and he did the job neatly. He exhibited few of the qualities which subsequently characterized his admittedly fine career as Governor.

In the years when the liberal movement was developing in both major parties, under Governor Woodrow Wilson of New Jersey and Governor Hiram Johnson of California, Al felt naught but contempt for all reformers.

"I would rather be a lamp post on Park Avenue," he growled to one who tried to interest him in advanced ideas, "than Governor of California."

For the years 1903–1918 Mr. Smith had his wish, insofar as he made any real contribution to the forces which were gathering throughout the world and the nation during that exciting period.

It was an accident—the Triangle fire—that transformed the young Tammany brave. That catastrophe brought a new and enduring influence into his life. During the legislative inquiry into sweatshops and industrial feudalism which followed the conflagration he was associated with Hebrew welfare workers of the metropolis.

From these human but hard-headed idealists he got an understanding of the social and political order contrasting sharply with that which he had been taught at Tammany Hall. From then on he grew rapidly. He who had once held government to be only a pawn in the game of politics now saw it as a social science. Soon he was sponsoring and passing the very reform measures which he used to kill at Mr. Murphy's behest.

Now he has escaped from all these early influences. He has passed into a period of Raskobian twilight.

Whether he can come back—whether there will be any call for him—is still to be determined by whatever forces shape our statesmen and our history.

It would be interesting, if no more, should he return to the political stage tempered by adversity —should he recapture and hold that spirit of humility and understanding which he showed that time he gazed awestruck at the log cabin in which

Abraham Lincoln was born. For when it was suggested that he capitalize the pilgrimage with a few words comparing his origin to that of the author of the Gettysburg Address, he replied angrily:

"Naw—nothin' to that idea. Abe Lincoln was a poor boy and so was I. But that doesn't make me a Lincoln by a long shot."

CALVIN COOLIDGE

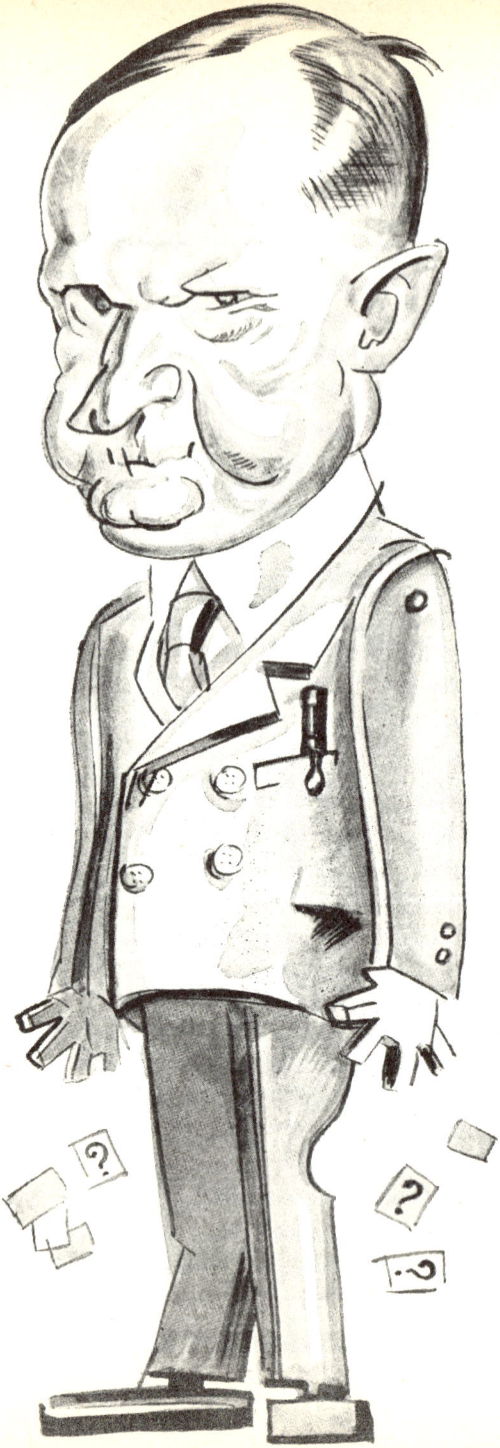

CALVIN COOLIDGE

The Presidency was a delightful daze and doze to Calvin Coolidge.

Concerning most problems which confronted his Administration he had not the slightest notion. Yet he never permitted his ignorance or incompetence to trouble his digestion of sausage and buckwheat cakes or those daily afternoon naps in the Executive Office. There was much of the Calvinist, a strong streak of religious and political fatalism, in his odd makeup.

A farm boy never doubts that the sun will rise —some day—and he was a farm boy.

Mr. Coolidge, whose solutions for the most serious problems assumed shape as neighborly common sense and old New England saws, drew on boyhood observation in dealing with domestic and foreign affairs of great magnitude. He knew that a little sunlight, a little rain, a little wind and a very little artificial cultivation raised the best crops—some

THE MIRRORS OF 1932

days. Blessed with golden weather during his occupancy of the White House, why toil and grub!

He knew, too, his Mellons.

His was the Negative Era and he was Negation personified. In a period when the American people wanted only to be let alone, to be free of Woodrow Wilson's incestuous idealism and even Warren Gamaliel Harding's Main Street immoralities, Providence sent them a Mr. Zero.

" 'Tain't so" was his attitude, life itself—toward almost all the verities except "spiritual values" at $2 a word and the Republican Party.

When Herbert Hoover, his eager young Secretary of Commerce, pestered Cabinet conferences with frantic suggestions that some troublesome problem might be disposed of through appointment of a "commission," Calvin would remark in a nasal drawl impossible of interpretation:

"Waal, might be a good thing. Might not. We'll see about thet lateh."

"Lateh" never came. Calvin always discovered, as he had guessed, that the effervescent engineer's fears were phantoms.

The incident reveals the fundamental difference between the Great Engineer and the Great Enigma.

CALVIN COOLIDGE

It is not surprising that Mr. Coolidge did not like Mr. Hoover. It is true that he permitted his Cabinet member to scheme for the presidential nomination while still a member of the Coolidgean household, thereby giving him an advantage over such lowly persons as Senators and ex-Governors, but the President eventually soured on his pushing protégé.

Calvin came to feel like the central figure in one of those New England tragedies of the countryside —like the ageing father whose eldest and least beloved son cannot conceal his impatience at the tenacity with which the old man clings to life.

In the last days of the pre-convention campaign Mr. Coolidge's attitude mystified even himself— which was not difficult. Although resentful against Mr. Hoover's importunities, he detested Charles G. Dawes, whose sleepiness on a certain day had caused Mr. Coolidge much mortification. Nor could he warm to the senatorial wishfuls—Messrs. Curtis, Watson, Willis and Goff—inasmuch as each had peeved him in the past.

Those who observed him during this travail derived a peculiar sense of satisfaction. They recalled that at Swampscott the only illustrious Republicans with whom he would not pose for a photograph were Mr. Dawes and Mr. Hoover. His solution of this personal dilemma, therefore, had all the elements of low comedy.

Exhibiting the elfin and mischievous spirit so characteristic of him, Mr. Coolidge played two pranks. The departing Polonius repaid the Capitol Hill coterie and his disloyal Vice-President by restraining them with his ambiguous "I do not choose" dictum until it was too late to head off the erstwhile Democrat, Mr. Hoover. Then Mr. Coolidge unloaded on an ungrateful party the one man in whom he had little political faith or confidence.

Pilgrims to the former President's two-room editorial sanctum, insurance office and legal headquarters at Northampton, Mass., discover that he is still Mr. Hoover's most cynical and observant critic.

"What's the wonder boy doin' now?" inquires Calvin.

Mr. Coolidge resents, in particular, his successor's effort to pose as a more thorough guardian of public monies than he was. The *Herald Tribune* columnist, whose recognition of his own limitations was his greatest source of strength, cannot endure it that he should be squeezed out of his economical niche in history. He guards that sacred spot as a dog would stand over his master's crypt. It is, he realizes, his political parsimony that may land him on the right side of historians' ledgers.

He shuddered from stem to stern when Mr. Hoover scrapped that presidential firetrap, the yacht *Mayflower,* which had given Mr. Coolidge so many adventurous moments on his half-mile cruises from the Washington Navy Yard to Haines Point. When Mr. Hoover, surpassing even his predecessor's prohibition of more substantial sanitation than paper cups and towels in the Executive Offices, shifted two unused riding horses from White House stables to Fort Myer, Mr. Coolidge remarked:

"Yes, I s'pose they'll eat less hay at the fort than they will at the White House."

Our foremost private citizen may, perhaps, be pardoned these wisecracks at the expense of the President of the United States. The Lord of Beechwood Manor, in contemplating bankrupt banks, slumped stocks and a panicky President, must seek ironic comfort in these unkind remarks for his unhappy role as America's Lost Legend.

It is, however, difficult to catch and to keep Mr. Coolidge in proper perspective. In retrospect—and in comparison—the Capital confers upon the little man the strength of a Washington, the philosophy of a Jefferson, the statesmanship of a Lincoln, the imagination of a Roosevelt and the ideals of a Woodrow Wilson. Yet none contends that he was a great Chief Executive, not even himself.

Myths are not easily destructible—and we need them so in these times—but for the sake of historical accuracy it must be set down that Mr. Coolidge was not the strong, silent figure a sycophantic press pictured him to be. He was, on the contrary, small and shabby—a crotchety, querulous, selfish and wearisomely loquacious. Withal, he was, personally, likable and readily understandable—an enigma only to unctuous and undiscerning folk.

I shudder to contemplate what might have been the nation's fate had a world crisis requiring real statesmanship beset his Administration. I sometimes think that Providence must watch over this Republican, if only negatively. Calvin was not made for his times so much as the times for him.

If he could evade a problem, he did—coal strikes, prohibition enforcement, oil scandals, mergers gone mad, the degradation of a major political party. To Mr. Hoover he bequeathed a legacy of social, economic and political ills rarely matched in the transfer of the Presidency. He knew, I think, that forces which he could not marshal were mobilizing throughout the nation and the world, and he was never wiser than in his abdication.

In those last days he was wont to dismiss problems laid on his neatly cleared desk with the comment: "We'll leave that to the wonder boy."

It is no accident that his skimping and deafness to demands for expansion necessitated a $10,000,000,000 Congress—the most costly in peace-time history—in his successor's first two years.

Mr. Coolidge has said that "the United States is about like the Second Ward in Northampton." So it was to him, and he operated on the scale of a smug ward boss. He swapped and traded shamelessly. He was ruthless, callous and selfish. He was quite without civic conscience. Thus he named a trust-builder to be Attorney General, a Pennsylvanian with sectional railroad interests to be a member of the Interstate Commerce Commission, a sugar baron to serve on the United States Tariff Commission. He had a conscience but it was uncoded—morals but no ethical sense.

Every man had his price, in Mr. Coolidge's opinion, though he never paid in actual cash. When a Senator opposed his policies or appointments, he made no fuss. Even the great William E. Borah failed to stir the presidential pulse by so much as an extra beat. There was never a sign that Calvin was aware of recalcitrancy. He simply marked time and his man. There would soon be a breakfast or a conference, and if the fellow's price were not too high, Mr. Coolidge met it. He never thought it worth while to try to bribe Mr. Borah, and therefore ignored him, with marked success. He never bullied or browbeat his foes; he fought or negotiated in the dark and in whispers. Similarly, he tempered defeat and reverses by unostentatious acceptance of the inevitable. He ate more heartily and slept more soundly on the very nights when his enemies remained awake to celebrate their triumph or to plan for the morrow's clash. And he grinned in his sleep.

Even in important affairs of state he utilized this crossroads, bargaining process. When France showed no inclination to refund its debt, Mr. Coolidge barred private loans to our former ally. When Mexico refused to rescind confiscatory land laws, he lifted the embargo on arms. It mattered not that most of the property involved was owned by that eminent patrioteer, Edward L. Doheny. When European nations broke up the 1926 arms conference, thereby blasting his desire to be known as the post-war pacificator, he permitted that aggressive

Ambassador, Hugh Gibson, to leap into the prints with the warning that "Europe is drifting into war."

He dealt more kindly with the practical politicians; to him, a practical politician, they were the bone and sinew of the nation. It explains, perhaps, why they liked him so well and begged him to stand for a third term. "The organization," to which he was wholly indebted for his small portion of fame and fortune, was his guide and god; he knew no others.

In view of the political morality prevailing among bootlegging bosses in the North and partisan carpetbaggers in the south there could be but one outcome. The federal officials named by Mr. Coolidge are of a low order unexampled; poor Mr. Harding's shine by comparison. Coolidge was ever content to accept workable political standards; he did not deem it his job to better them.

Calvin was neither a leader nor an executive. He was a manipulator.

In Mr. Coolidge's abject worship of wealth lies the key to his whole Administration. His was not the deep, definite faith in the going and golden order Mr. Hoover exhibits. It was, rather, an almost touching awe and suppressed envy of those who

THE MIRRORS OF 1932

have what money will buy. Such an attitude was only natural. Until he became Vice-President his social and financial state was that of a middle-class struggler.

None too successful as a lawyer, he had never earned more than a few thousand dollars a year before he came to the Capital. It was not his spirit of simplicity, as his subsequent craving for creature comforts showed, that led him to live in a $32.50 house in Northampton. He could afford no better. At Boston he occupied two dark and drab rooms in an old-fashioned, downtown hotel. Upon his arrival at Washington he was amazed to discover that his $15,000-a-year salary would not permit himself to establish his family in a dwelling, and he took a suite at the Willard Hotel.

There was little improvement in his estate even then. He was a "singed cat." Alice Longworth, who heard the witticism at her dentist's, said he "looked as if he had been weaned on a pickle." Society tried to take him up, discovered neither humor nor humility in him, and soon lost interest.

"Mister Vice-President," said a charming dinner companion, hoping to make conversation, "I have just bet that I can make you talk."

CALVIN COOLIDGE

"You lose," he snapped, and gazed, with clamped lips, straight ahead all evening.

The Senate mocked and made sport of him; its rowdiness appalled him. Audiences jeered or walked out on this outlandish figure when he essayed to serve as the Administration's Prince of Wales. The politicians were scheming to drop him at the expiration of Mr. Harding's term. But they reckoned without his luck—luck so extraordinary that his nomination for the vice-presidency was humorously reported to have induced Mr. Harding to double his life insurance policy.

Mr. Coolidge was a trivial person, and these trivialities deeply affected his Administration. As President, he snubbed the Senate which had scorned him and the society which had ignored him. Out of gratitude for kindnesses shown him by Senator and Mrs. Frank B. Kellogg he made "Nervous Nellie" Secretary of State in an era destined to see the settlement of grave international problems. The Kelloggs, taking pity on the Coolidges, paid a call on the Vice-President at the Willard. They found the Coolidges lonesome and tearful. When Calvin entered the White House, no longer friendless and forlorn, he did not forget this kindly gesture.

THE MIRRORS OF 1932

In the presence of Andrew W. Mellon—who represented wealth—and Charles Evans Hughes—who had brains—Mr. Coolidge permitted his inferiority complex to paralyze him. He accepted orders from "Uncle Andy" and lectures from Mr. Hughes. He was canny enough to realize that the Pittsburgh banker symbolized happy days to a money-mad generation. It was Mellon who juggled figures and dumped golden gifts on Calvin's desk, but it was the latter who possessed the astuteness to make a Mosaic law of the prosperity slogan.

There were times, indeed, when the two tiny figures resembled a pair of modern Midases blindly groping to transform whatever they touched into political currency.

Their partisan greed eventually undid them. These two prophets of perennial prosperity were caught quite unaware by the faint rumblings recorded on Wall Street seismographs in May of 1928. They knew, of course, that it would not do to permit a crash until Mr. Coolidge had slipped away from the scenes of golden glory. The two thereupon hit on a smart but questionable device for maintaining price levels.

The process was simple; it was prosperity by political proclamation. If the stock ticker showed a slump at Monday closing or Tuesday opening, Mr. Coolidge invariably devoted his Tuesday noon press conference to bullish statements. "Don't sell America short," was their tenor. If the market's fluctuation necessitated it, he did it again on Friday afternoon.

When the President was not, like a Colossus, holding up prices, Mr. Mellon, of a Tuesday morning or Thursday afternoon, took over the task. Thus, for almost a year, the two promoted the movement of money into speculative channels, and thereby accentuated the crash which blew up the Hoover Administration.

I would not be surprised if Mr. Hoover's prejudice against Mr. Mellon sprang from a realization of the poor service the Secretary of the Treasury had done the incoming Administration. It is another example of Mr. Coolidge's sagacity that, unlike Mr. Mellon, he retired in his political prime. I think he would be glad to return, however, if he could be assured that those golden days would return with him. Another condition he might impose—and Republicans would undoubtedly agree to it—is that he be permitted to keep his sidelines as a columnist and an insurance executive. The allure of the White House is strong, and no recent

President revelled in its personal and official perquisites and prerogatives more than Calvin.

Mr. Coolidge's taciturnity was simply temperament. I have seen men shift from one foot to another in an effort to relieve the physical and mental strain of listening while he talked on and on—and said nothing. His secretaries often complained that he mussed up his morning engagement list by prolonging his appointments out of a desire to "have a chat." On *Mayflower* trips he constituted himself as a guide and gave his guests no rest. His favorite joke was, as the vessel slipped by Alexandria on the Potomac River, to recall that its inhabitants once dreamed it might become a greater seaport than New York. He remained above deck until he had cackled over the frustrated hopes of people 100 years dead, and then he disappeared below, yachting cap and all. But if others tried to open a conversation with him, he froze. A slick actor, he knew that he could not step out of his role as "Calvin the Silent," and in his public appearances and statements he economized on words. It was his only economy, however, and, like his other ventures along this line, purely political.

He was an inveterate gossip. Resenting the barrier erected about his precious person, he kept his ears open. He heard everything and knew everything, whether it was the birth of a nation or the prospective birth of Alice Longworth's baby. Almost every morning, while awaiting the delivery of the White House newspaper order—the *Washington Post,* the New York *Times,* the New York *Herald Tribune* and the Philadelphia *Public Ledger*—he exchanged small talk with correspondents or the police guard in the outer Executive Office. He had a rare capacity for obtaining knowledge without exhibiting interest, for getting information without giving any.

An anecdote illustrates this trait. It is one of those stories that is truer than history, even though the incident may be only imaginary. Sitting one evening in the upstairs study, his head deep in a newspaper, he seemed to be paying no attention to a discussion between Mrs. Coolidge and Mrs. Stearns. They had just learned that Mrs. Longworth was to have a baby, and, womanlike, their next concern was the date of its birth. Their interest was quite pardonable. It was, being the Longworth's first baby after nineteen years of marriage, more than a "blessed event"; it was national in character. Calvin, however, seemed to give no heed, but his ears were pricked. When the ladies were about to leave it to Providence, the President interposed.

"January 14," he snapped, without raising his eyes from his page.

He was only a month off.

Through conscientious reading the newspapers he kept himself informed. Unlike Mr. Hoover, who scans carefully clipped accounts from 1,500 newspapers, Mr. Coolidge read with middle-class curiosity and carelessness—international articles, domestic stories, editorials, the social column, financial lists, want ads. He caught therein the authentic voice, prejudices, pleasures, trends—and votes—of the people. Never did Mr. Coolidge have to ask, as did Mr. Hoover, "Who is Rudy Vallée?" I often think that the little Vermonter's political wisdom was due to his daily dip into the newspaper columns.

Mr. Coolidge was a great thinker—or at least he went through the mental motions. Attachés at the White House say that the "never worked." Of a morning he might be found peering through the trees at his favorite source of inspiration—the cold shaft of the Washington Monument. On frosty days he preferred to stand, hands clasped behind his back, against the blazing fireplace in his circular office chamber. After dinner, which was served at noon, he napped, and his head hardly touched the pillow before he was snoring. At four o'clock, if business was not pressing—and it rarely was—he napped again, his feet propped on his desk. Often he stole off to the White House late of an afternoon for a more comfortable doze, his coat, vest and shoes removed. Between 9 and 10, concluding an evening of snoozing or silent companionship with Mrs. Coolidge and the Stearnses, he headed for bed.

The White House, indeed, meant little more than good board and room to Calvin.

There was, withal, purpose behind this laziness and procrastination. Mr. Coolidge possessed the true spirit of an executive. Cabinet officers who would turn their problems over to him got a sharp lecture. "Jimmie" Davis, whose brass and bonhomerie doubtless aroused amused contempt in the restrained Mr. Coolidge, was the first to suffer such a rebuke. When "Jimmie" breathless but beaming, bounded in on Mr. Coolidge soon after the latter took office, the President asked if the Secretary of Labor had found an answer to his problem.

"Why, no, Mister President," replied Davis, taken aback. "I thought we'd get together, talk it over and see what could be done."

THE MIRRORS OF 1932

"Waal," drawled Calvin. "That's what you're paid for. When you know what you want to do, you come to me. Don't ever come in again this-away."

This harsh treatment might have been due, in part, to his dislike of the Davis sort of fellow. Calvin liked simple, unpretentious folk. He joked and played pranks with his Secret Service guards. He borrowed money from them to buy a magazine or a newspaper. He payed it back with the same ritual that accompanies refunding of the national debt. On one occasion he despatched an emergency call for Richard Jervis, head of the White House Secret Service staff. Poor "Dick," horror-stricken lest a plot against the President's life might have been frustrated during his absence, scurried into Mr. Coolidge's office. Without lifting his head from the document he was inditing, the President held out a dime and a nickel to "Dick."

It was a half-hour later that Jervis recalled he had, several weeks before, loaned the President fifteen cents on one of their morning walks.

"Better wear your rubbers," said Calvin one fine morning as he met his Secret Service escort on the White House threshold.

To protests that the sun was shining, and the

ground dry, Mr. Coolidge repeated: "Better wear your rubbers."

Upon returning to the White House the President noted a cupful of rain-water hemmed within a rut in the road.

"See," he said triumphantly as he turned to the Secret Service man trudging along heavily. "Told you you'd better wear your rubbers."

Curiosity and mischievousness were mingled in him. Passing the police sentry box in front of the White House, he noted a bell there. Upon pressing it, he observed it brought another policeman on a trot from the guardrooms 100 yards away. Thereafter, Calvin frequently pushed the bell, and, disappearing within the White House, he peeked through the curtains to watch the results. The bell-ringing may have been but curiosity the first time, but, so his closeup critics think, it was a form of sadism thereafter.

There was, I believe, a satiric slyness in him. What else would induce him to torture a friend as he did when the latter visited Mr. Coolidge while he was Vice-President.

"Will you have a little drink?" asked Calvin.

The friend, somewhat shocked at the thought that the Vice-President would violate the prohibition law beneath the Capitol Dome, concealed his surprise and volunteered that he would.

Whereupon, Mr. Coolidge moved toward a miniature refrigerator. As he stooped to open it, he inquired:

"What'll it be—white rock or ginger ale?"

In all these gleeful emprises, however, Mr. Coolidge exhibited no spirit of playfulness. For him the fun rested in the puzzlement of his victims. He himself, he recognized, was the joke, and not what he did or said. As President, he sensed that he was a "character," and, as such, occupied a distinct place in the American scene. Truly humble, surprised at his own success, he was content to escape from the White House with a whole skin and, for him, a fortune.

He is, without a doubt, happier now than ever before in his career. He can doze without his daze being discovered. His retirement is in keeping with his character. What President in modern times has turned from a stirring world stage to such bucolic peace and obscurity! Roosevelt hunted in Africa, Taft took a chair at Yale, Wilson dreamed on and died, Harding descended unto dust.

Mr. Coolidge snoozes and sits, resting on his morals.

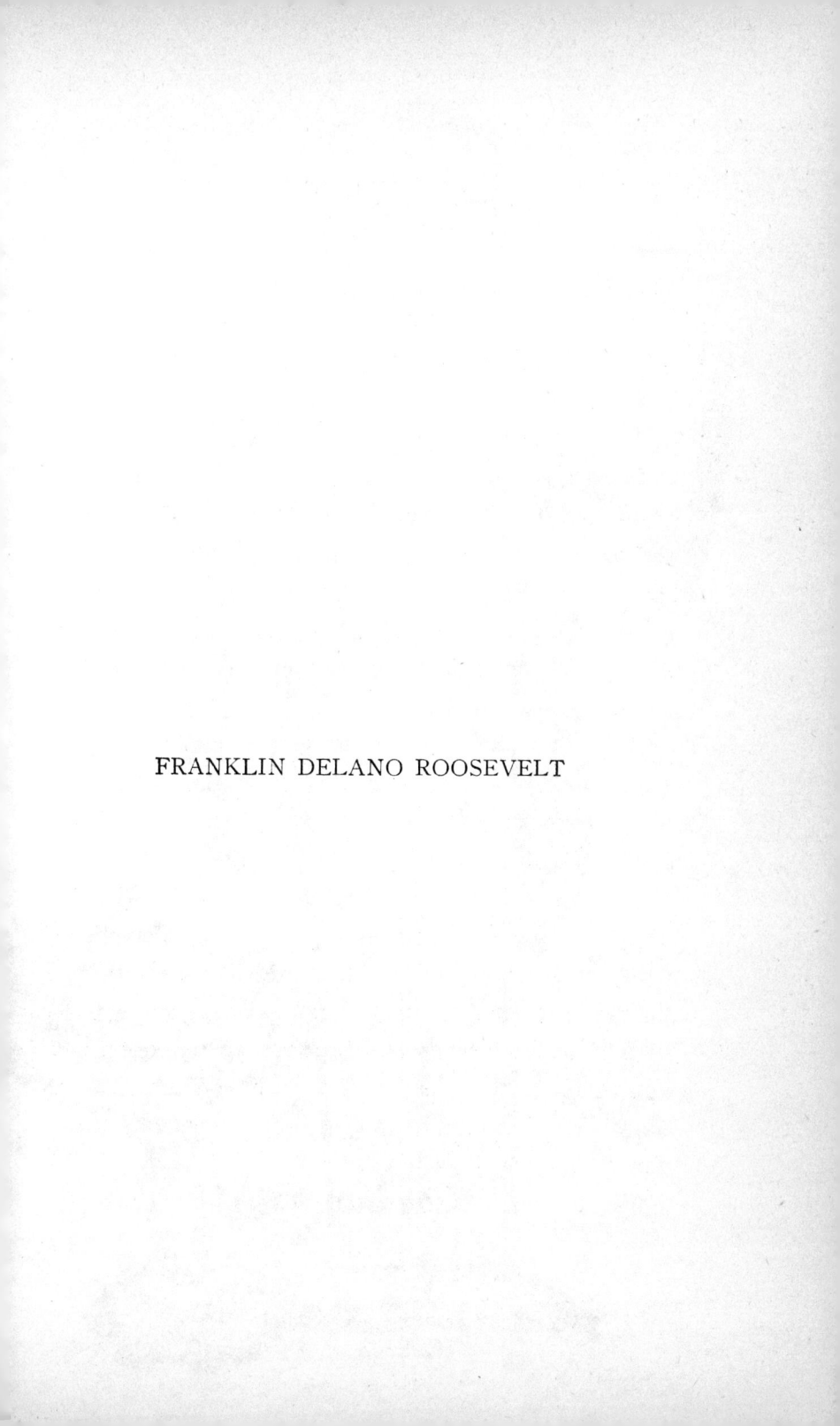

FRANKLIN DELANO ROOSEVELT

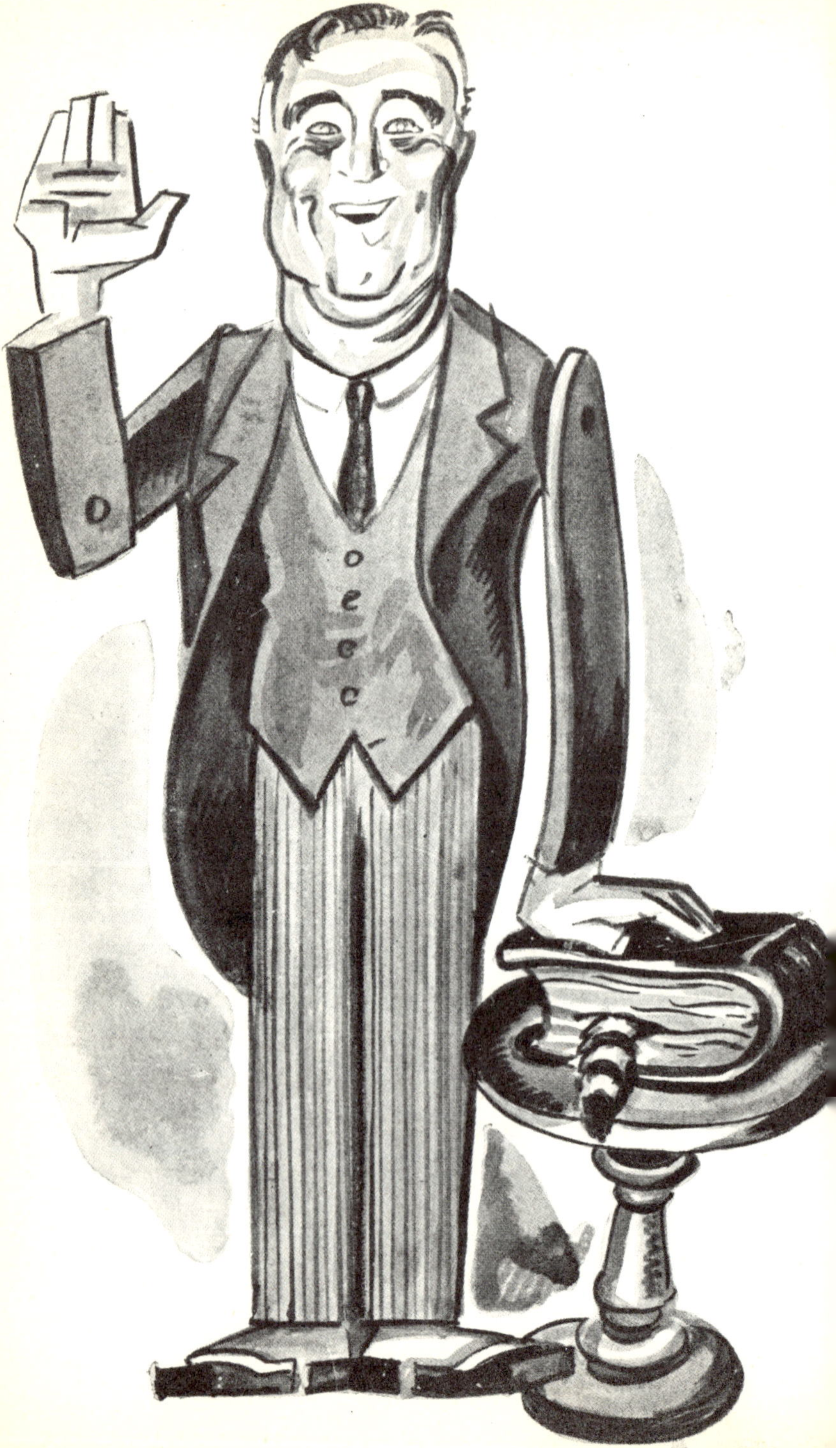

FRANKLIN D. ROOSEVELT

Franklin D. Roosevelt has been pushed into almost everything he has ever done.

He has the heart, he has the head—with some reservations—but he lacks guts.

Having said this about the Groton-Harvard-Columbia Governor of New York, who has taken to telling rough stories in an awkward effort to be a regular guy, the rest of this chapter is unnecessary.

However—

The fifth cousin of Theodore the First is an excellent example of what a conspicuous name will do for a man in politics. Were he a Smith or a Baker or a Robinson, he would have dropped from sight and sound years ago.

But this distant and Democratic member of the Roosevelt family, despite childish spats with the Republican tribe, has made the most of his name. He has pawned it out for political use by such grotesquely irreconcilable factions as the reform element in New York, the Wilson Administration, the McAdooites, Al Smith's one-man circus and Tammany Hall.

Although it has become slightly shopworn and tarnished through all these transactions, now he means to trade on it himself—perhaps to redeem it.

He looks to be the best of the Democratic presidential lot, to be sure, but he does not stand up so well under close scrutiny.

Although advanced as a liberal—the most vociferous one among the candidates of the major parties—his liberalism is born of impulse rather than intelligence or conviction. It moves him, except when he can see a definite gain in sight, only slowly and sporadically.

He is indecisive, indiscreet and impulsive. Ever ready to embrace the newest fad or figure in politics, he surrenders himself wholeheartedly to momentary men and issues. Thus he has shifted and swerved through vicissitudinous years to serve such antipathetic leaders as Woodrow Wilson, William G. McAdoo, Alfred E. Smith and John F. Curry.

He needs balance and ballast.

Expediency rules him. He wavers between warring sets of advisers. Those who have his ear last usually prevail.

FRANKLIN D. ROOSEVELT

Through some vagary in his nature, he cannot stay put. He is not dependable. Political correspondents at Albany do not trust him, although they like him. When it seems wise, he leaves them out on a limb. He denies and deserts them whenever he deems it necessary.

In his first formal speech for the nomination he gave a sample of the sort of candidate—and President—he might be. He forgot to deliver the diatribe against the Hoover Administration found in advance copies of his address, and then explained that he was "not conscious of having left anything out."

He's the same old Roosevelt Washington knew twenty-five years ago. This was one of T. R.'s favorite tricks for getting his ideas across without assuming responsibility for them.

The politicians find it difficult to keep up with the New York Governor from hour to hour, although he rarely gives them serious discomfort. He may fidget but he does not get far away from them. He is too much in their debt, and he hopes the debt will be larger by 1932.

His heart, more often than not, is in the right place, but he cannot coordinate his head—or his latter-day ambitions. He cannot concentrate, and problems requiring serious study and persistent plugging leave him cold. He diffuses his great store of nervous energy in leaping from one idea to another. His physical handicap apparently needs compensation in mental activity.

He draws support from so many rival factions that he defies definition. He is idolized by Tammany Hall, yet he is the favorite of those who despise the New York Democrats. He is the darling of the men with whom he served during the Wilson Administration, but he has few enemies among anti-Wilson politicians. Although he has, belatedly, become converted to the wet cause, the drys have little fear of him.

He has, like Herbert Hoover, taken his friends where and as he found them. Should he become President, he cannot satisfy them all. It would, indeed, be a bad day for the Democratic Party should he sit in the White House. He might easily become the same sort of disrupting influence that Mr. Hoover is in the Republican Party.

Wets and drys, liberals and reactionaries, Wilsonian idealists and machine bosses, Tammany and Bible Belt Democrats—all rally around him. It is characteristic that each coterie claims him.

The answer is that Mr. Roosevelt, once a dry

FRANKLIN D. ROOSEVELT

and a liberal and a reformer, has listed with every political wind that has blown within the last twenty years. He has stood in every camp; he has fought on every firing line.

He is the soldier of fortune of American politics.

All these allegiances prove both a help and a hindrance now.

Yet this fine chap is no conscious hypocrite or dissembler. He is, according to his lights, honest and sincere, and surely well-meaning. He undoubtedly believes that he remains faithful to the ideals with which he set out to purify politics in the boss-ridden State of New York in 1910.

The truth is that Mr. Roosevelt, a cultured and conscientious fellow, aspires to be the glorious Galahad of politics that he has been represented to be. He likes to pose as a great liberal and reformist. His instincts and intelligence—even his prejudices—impel him in that direction. His record, for all its shiftiness and spottiness, shows a pitiful persistence to go along with the goo-goos.

This is the Roosevelt the public has seen; it is the only Roosevelt the public knows. It is the Roosevelt whom Tammany Hall will undoubtedly present to the Democrats as its presidential choice.

THE MIRRORS OF 1932

It is the Roosevelt whom Will Durant eulogized so ecstatically at the Houston convention.

"Here on the stage," Durant wrote, "was Franklin Roosevelt—beyond question the finest man that has appeared at either convention. Beside him the master minds who held the platform at Kansas City were crude bourgeois, porters suddenly made rich.

"A figure tall and proud, even in suffering; a face of classic profile, pale with years of struggle against paralysis; a frame nervous and yet self-controlled with that tense, taut unity of spirit which lifts the complex soul above those whose calmness is mere stolidity; most obviously a gentleman and a scholar, a man softened and cleansed and illumined with pain.

"This is a civilized man; he could look Balfour and Poincaré in the face. For the moment we are lifted up."

A "complex soul" he most certainly is. But I question whether there is a "tense, taut unity of spirit" in him.

Mr. Roosevelt no longer fits this fanciful frame, if he ever did. Now that he desires so to be President, he is no longer the same inspiring individual.

FRANKLIN D. ROOSEVELT

Even without this handicap, he could not be the shining figure which his friends—and Mr. Durant—picture.

He is, for one thing, too intense, too impetuous, too indecisive. He attaches himself to a cause or a personality without deliberation, and stubborn loyalty even to a bad cause or a dominant personality thereafter blinds and betrays him. His unquestioning loyalties—to Mr. Wilson, to Mr. McAdoo, to Mr. Smith, and now to Tammany Hall—quite undermine his reputation either for greatness or goodness.

He is a political cavorter. The Republican Roosevelts call him a "maverick."

Consider his career–

Embracing the so-called Wilsonian idealism as Assistant Secretary of the Navy, this liberal let himself be used as an exponent of warlike imperialism on the western hemisphere. Indeed, he boasted that he wrote the Haitian Constitution, and he directed the marines' invasion of that unhappy island.

When war or peace hung in the balance, he announced that our fleet was sufficiently strong to conquer Mexico. He rivalled the Kaiser in rattling the saber.

THE MIRRORS OF 1932

In his 1920 campaign for the vice-presidency he first declared, and subsequently denied, that our dominance in South and Central America was such as to force those nations to vote with us if we joined the League of Nations.

He became an apostle of compulsory and universal military training. He was a mercurial Martian. He visited Smedley Butler's bastard-bastion in Haiti soon after its capture, he travelled on a destroyer to Europe, he could barely be restrained from enlisting as an ordinary gob.

He was, in those exciting days, a brave and boisterous fellow—and an honest one. He was, too, an able Assistant Secretary of the Navy. He simply permitted his equilibrium to be unbalanced by the intensity of his devotion to Woodrow Wilson.

He was even then a liberal, or so he thought, but it might be asked what virtue there is in the liberal heart which cannot keep its head when all other liberals go mad! His liberalism—alas!—becomes lost or lame under the fire of friendship or emotion. It becomes twisted in the bright, boyish heat of his impulses.

His dilly-dallying with the prohibition issue is characteristic.

FRANKLIN D. ROOSEVELT

For years he was a prohibitionist through principle. No hard liquor passed his lips or his threshold. In 1911 he sponsored the first local option measure brought to Albany by the Anti-Saloon League, lending himself to the movement that was climaxed by the Eighteenth Amendment and the Volstead Act.

As late as the spring of 1930 he refused to see that prohibition was unpopular. He ventured the opinion that a national referendum would disclose the country to be dry. He was a dry when he nominated Al Smith, an arch-repealer, in 1924 and in 1928.

He shifted, however, simultaneously with indications that the wets were gaining ground, and that a white-ribboner could not win the Democratic presidential nomination.

Despite this conversion, he secretly mobilized southern drys against National Chairman John J. Raskob's simple demand that the National Committee consider the question of repeal of the dry laws. Publicly, he declined to intervene with the explanation that it was a national rather than a State problem. Privately, he sent hysterical telegrams to southern Democrats urging them to oppose the Raskob-Smith program.

THE MIRRORS OF 1932

His conduct in this party crisis did him little credit.

He is, it appears, just another politician—just another Roosevelt.

He has rushed in where angels fear to tread, yet he would have us believe that his wings have not been singed. He would have us think that he is still the same, unsoiled, unspoiled "college kid candidate" that he was when he broke into the political game twenty years ago.

Perhaps he is. In any event, it is hard to dislike this Roosevelt—or any Roosevelt.

It is also difficult to destroy the myth that all Roosevelt males are great and good men. It is impossible to suggest at this stage that even Theodore Roosevelt was a trimmer, a theatrical fellow, a sound rather than a force on many occasions. Yet those enjoying even a remote acquaintance with New York or national politics have few illusions anent the founder of the political line.

"If Roosevelt were not a coward," said one of his associates at Albany—the late Tom Grady—"he would have been the greatest man in the world."

The same comment, *in parvo,* applies to this littler Roosevelt.

Mr. Grady, a famous Tammany spell-binder,

FRANKLIN D. ROOSEVELT

may have been inexact in his definitions. The Roosevelts cannot be defined or defamed so succintly. Nevertheless, there is as much braggadocio as bravery in their makeup, more of indecision than independence, opportunism strangely mingled with idealism.

These elements, although diluted and dissipated in his relatives and descendants, were so mingled in the elder Teddy that the world pronounced him "a man."

The same sort of political chemistry has produced Franklin D. Roosevelt. And it is difficult to dislike him.

He has never fought ferociously or unfairly. There is no indignation in him. In fact, even his friends hint, that except for a certain streak of slow stubbornness, he will not battle for his beliefs at all. When he was opposing Charles F. Murphy at Albany, he was sipping beer and exchanging confidences with the Tammany dictator's spokesmen— Al Smith, Senator Robert F. Wagner and Mr. Grady.

It throws a great light on Mr. Roosevelt to discover that, for all his warfare against Tammany Hall, those politicians-for-revenue-only now exalt him above either Mr. Smith or Senator Wagner.

THE MIRRORS OF 1932

No man animated and activated by the ideals and independence attributed to Franklin D. Roosevelt could bob up, as he does, astride the Tiger instead of inside the animal.

The Tammany sachems are vindictive men, never forgetting or forgiving. They have driven Mr. Smith, their erstwhile leader and Mr. Roosevelt's own "Happy Warrior," from the Wigwam.

Yet they dream of making Mr. Roosevelt the next President of the United States.

Washington is to be their happy hunting ground and the Governor of New York their Great and Good White Father.

Mr. Roosevelt's early political record has been forgotten in the rush of his more recent achievements, but it cannot be passed over in any proper estimate of him. The facts alone show him to be a remarkable man; they show why Tammany is not afraid of him.

A few years out of Harvard, where, as editor of the *Crimson,* he shocked staid university trustees with editorial demands for "dormitory fire escapes," he stood as a candidate for the Assembly for the Dutchess County district. No Democrat had been elected there in three decades, but premonitory signs of revolt encouraged him.

FRANKLIN D. ROOSEVELT

The Progressives were coming, and Theodore was home from Africa, Rome and way stations.

Although the collegian rode around in a newfangled automobile, wore tailor-made suits and smoked cigarettes, he was elected. His platform denounced bossism, but it is probable that his promise to enact a law standardizing apple barrels had more to do with his victory than his denunciations of Mr. Murphy and Tammany.

He arrived at Albany at an opportune moment for a young man ambitious to make a name for himself. The Legislature, a few days before, had got orders from the Tammany boss to elect "Blue-Eyed Billie" Sheehan as United States Senator to succeed Chauncey M. Depew. Mr. Sheehan was the candidate of the public utilities and the railroads, but the horrible fact that he was the personal choice of Mr. Murphy seemed to influence Mr. Roosevelt most.

For more than sixty ballots he and a handful of up-State Democrats stalemated the contest. Like himself, his associates had been elected from normally Republican strongholds, and they had little to lose by their defiance of dictation. Aligned against the Rooseveltian amateurs in this struggle were Mr. Smith and Senator Wagner, who were then tools of the machine, but the "young Harvard fellow" retained their friendship even as he fought them, and wrung a compromise from the boss.

This clash, coming at a time when there was a growing demand for popular election of Senators, won Mr. Roosevelt no little notoriety. It was not, of course, generally realized that the dispute, despite the young Assemblyman's honorable part in it, actually involved a rivalry between two great financial interests—the Ryan-Belmont crowd represented by Sheehan and the Morgan group represented by the opposing candidate, Edward F. Shepherd.

Mr. Roosevelt again fought Tammany at Baltimore. He went to that historic convention as organizer of the Empire State Democracy and committed to the candidacy of Woodrow Wilson. While Mr. Murphy voted his delegation, including young Al Smith, Messrs. Ryan and Belmont, with sullen steadiness for Champ Clark, Mr. Roosevelt lobbied for the Princeton academician.

In taking over the government, President Wilson discovered the Democrats to be lamentably lacking in Cabinet material. He even appointed Josephus Daniels, a South Carolina editor, to be Secretary of the Navy, and Daniels was the one

FRANKLIN D. ROOSEVELT

man upon whom Mr. Roosevelt had made a deep impression at Baltimore. So Daniels asked "that nice young fellow," as he referred to the New York man, to be his assistant.

Although Mr. Roosevelt was periodically advanced as an anti-Tammany candidate for Governor, he preferred to remain at Washington. There he headed the hopeless movement inspired by Mr. McAdoo to raise up an office-holding clique in New York as a rival to Tammany Hall. For eight years Mr. Roosevelt advised on policies and appointments designed to weaken or destroy the regular, anti-Wilson machine in the metropolis.

During his years at the Capital he became a popular favorite. Then in full possession of his health, he was an attractive figure—tall, broad-shouldered, blue-eyed, curly-haired. He was invariably described as sweet, able, active, amiable; he was a Don Quixote in politics. Indeed, he was one of the few sub-Cabinet members of the Wilson Administration to gain much credit for his services.

He made influential friends among local dowagers, national politicians and newspaper correspondents.

It availed him naught in New York, however.

THE MIRRORS OF 1932

In 1914 he contested for the senatorial nomination against James W. Gerard, and was badly beaten. He abused both Mr. Gerard and Mr. Murphy in language hardly to be expected of so cultured a chap.

His subsequent conduct was unexplainable. He announced that he would support Mr. Gerard if the latter would renounce Mr. Murphy and all his works. Mr. Gerard did not take this advice, but Mr. Roosevelt supported him.

Despite his brawls with the political boys and bosses, he is noted for his regularity once the convention—or the party pooh-bah—has passed upon platforms and candidates.

This trait may explain, in part, why Tammany, as well as other factions in his party, have no concern lest he prove revolutionary or unrewarding should he reach the White House. He considers himself a regular. He described his democracy in these earlier days in the following terms:

"I am a regular organization Democrat of Dutchess County, a New York State Democrat and a National Democrat.

"I am not an anti-Tammany Democrat, but in this campaign, as in many others, I have taken a consistent position against control of the State's

FRANKLIN D. ROOSEVELT

Democracy by Charles Francis Murphy, believing that he is a menace to our Democracy."

In the light of this declaration, his behaviour at the San Francisco convention in 1920 was both amusing and puzzling. There was not much consistency in him then.

Along with Samuel Seabury and a few others he dreamed that the invalided Woodrow Wilson might be renominated—evidence of his misreading of the times and trends—and then shifted to Mr. McAdoo as Wilson's heir. When Mr. Murphy's men sat resentfully in their seats, refusing to participate in a demonstration to the War President, the devoted Mr. Roosevelt tore the New York standard from Tammany hands and headed the parade around the hall.

It was dramatic and Rooseveltian, but Tammany's candidate—James M. Cox—was nominated in rebuke to the McAdoo wing. Mr. Roosevelt did not accept it as such, however, and soon fell into the arms of Mr. Murphy.

Although the Assistant Secretary of the Navy knew that he was to be presented as the vice-presidential candidate, he leaped to the stage to nominate Al Smith for that office. Beneath the platform the bosses were even then completing arrangements for him to be Mr. Cox's running-mate, and when he was placed in nomination by Mr. Smith, he consented to team up with Tammany's wet presidential candidate.

Mr. Murphy, knowing that the ticket was doomed to defeat, grinned. He had, he sensed, caught a Roosevelt. It was an excellent bargain for the boss—an empty vice-presidential nomination that might, and did, remove an enemy from the far more important field of New York politics.

The less said about Mr. Roosevelt's campaign, the better. He had the Democratic ticket in trouble from the moment he took the stump with his extravagant charges and language. He made the League of Nations his principal issue. He exhibited a surprising sensitiveness that distracted attention from his more serious purposes.

His tour of the nation was strewn with statements and denials and bitter exchanges with politicians, editors and correspondents. He had once again become too intense, too impetuous, too indiscreet. He was, obviously, beyond his depth.

He soon dropped from sight, and he might have remained in obscurity had not Al Smith resurrected him. Recognizing the value of the name of Roosevelt, Al got him to present the humble name of Smith to the 1924 convention. In the bloody and brooding atmosphere of Madison Square Garden he pleaded with the Democrats to take "this man of destiny whom our State proudly dedicates to the nation."

Again Mr. Roosevelt was intense, even imperious—and this time inspiring. Again he made a lasting impression even upon those who disagreed with him. He was, sitting in his wheel chair, a brave and gallant figure. At Houston in 1928 he repeated his plea, this time victoriously.

Came September and Al needed him as a candidate for Governor of New York to strengthen the national ticket. But from Warm Springs, Georgia, there was voiced a pathetic refusal. Mr. Roosevelt wired:

"My physicians are very definite in stating that the continued improvement in my walking is dependent on my avoiding the cold climate of winter and taking the exercises here in the winter months. It probably means getting rid of my leg braces within the next two years, and that would be impossible at Albany."

Mr. Roosevelt finally acquiesced—and there can

be no gainsaying the unselfishness of the sacrifice, even though he was catapulted to the top and Al sank out of sight.

As Governor, Mr. Roosevelt has made a good record. He has continued and expanded along the lines by which his predecessor transformed New York from a mediaeval to a modern State.

Out of a desire to be his own man rather than a shadow he has thrown Mr. Smith's friends and the latter's great water-power policy out the window. Sensing that he must have an issue of his own, the Governor had no qualms at breaking with Mr. Smith on this question.

It reflects the general cleavage between Mr. Roosevelt and his political godfather. It also indicates that Mr. Roosevelt prefers to preserve an issue rather than solve a problem.

The innately conservative Mr. Smith simply proposed, in dealing with power, that the State construct generating plants. Mr. Roosevelt, however, felt the need of a more advanced and attractive program. Since the Smith plan had been before the people for many years, the issues involved therein had lost their political potency.

Mr. Roosevelt wanted sharper weapons and found them. He proposed that the State enter the

FRANKLIN D. ROOSEVELT

busines of transmission of power provided it could not conclude "satisfactory" contracts with private distributors. But he neglected to define what he would regard as "satisfactory" arrangements, and he has failed to provide for his alternative of public transmission lines.

His proposal, moreover, is an invasion of private industry which Mr. Smith would not countenance. It explains, perhaps, why the Raskob-Young-Baruch group, although willing to accept the Smith program, regard Mr. Roosevelt as "socialistic."

Mr. Roosevelt's more visionary ideas have gained him friends among the Norris-La Follette Progressives, but it appears that his predecessor's is the more practical program. The Governor's is apparently inspired by sound politics rather than sound economics.

In his relations with Tammany Hall Mr. Roosevelt equivocates. He cannot get the nomination without the organization's indorsement, but he cannot win if he rides the Tiger instead of the Donkey. It is in his effort to keep his balance between the two animals that he may suffer a fall. He cannot convince the country that he is another Grover Cleveland if he continues to shadow-box with erring district leaders in New York.

THE MIRRORS OF 1932

If there is some pretense in his relations with the metropolitan machine, there is none in his contacts with country folk. Whereas most Democratic Governors of New York neglect the "hick" voters, he cultivates them. He once wrote to an urban friend that "you don't breed the kind of people we do in the country, although (the Roosevelt strain again) you breed good people."

His rural ties and sympathies are real. They are a distinct asset, and they may assert themselves nationally as they did when he carried the agricultural sections of his own State. Since almost any Democrat should win the cities against Mr. Hoover, this appeal to the country people may give him just the advantage he will need if he and Mr. Hoover are the 1932 set-ups.

The Democrats will also count on his ancestral name to land him in the White House. So does Mr. Roosevelt. He considers himself the greatest and grandest of all the tribe.

"You see," he once said in telling of his interest in forestry, "T. R. was the Roosevelt who chopped down trees.

"I am the Roosevelt who plants them."

DWIGHT WHITNEY MORROW

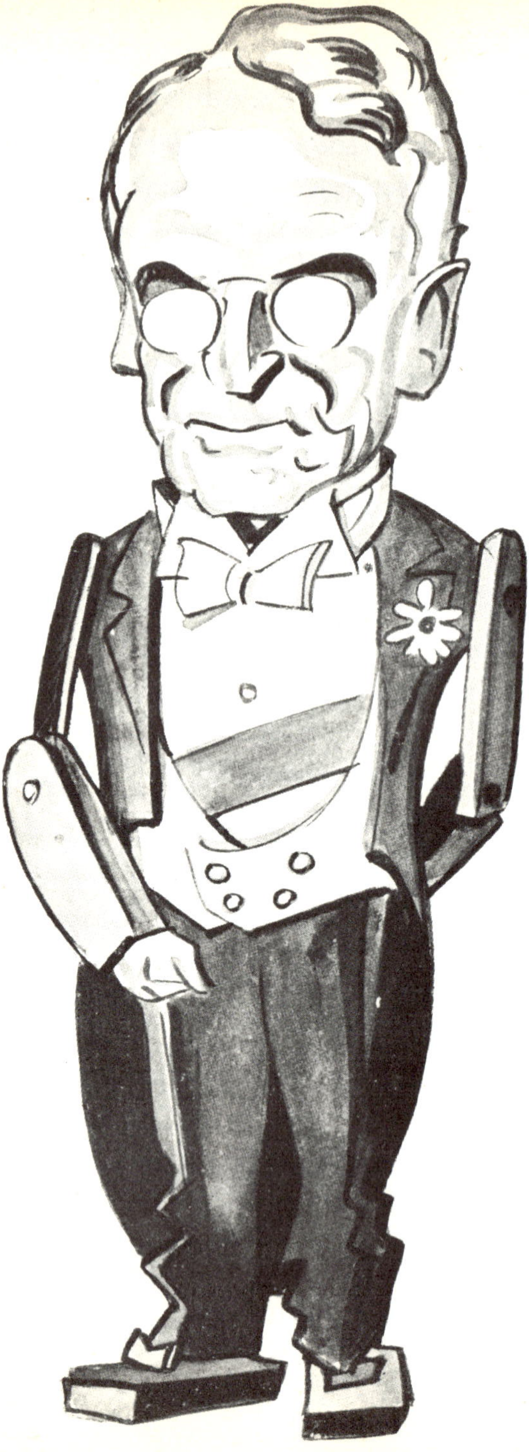

DWIGHT WHITNEY MORROW

Dwight Whitney Morrow is the poor little rich boy of American politics.

He always wanted to pursue an aimless, academic career, to be a literary or pedagogic figure, but now that he has moved from the House of Morgan to the House of Congress, he finds the political annex to his old institution of learning a dull place.

He fears that he has made a bad bargain—his first—and that he has sold himself, not only short, but to the very lowest bidder. Having manipulated the golden strings to which political puppets dance for so long, he suffers not from the delusions of grandeur of the run-of-mine Senator.

Personally, he is unhappy and beset with the doubt that he may be miscast in the United States Senate. Its methods are not his, and they never will be. He is capable in action but diffident of speech; his colleagues are full-blown with orations, empty of ideas and craven in action.

Statesmen, even Presidents and Senators, are not the sort of men he expected them to be. Bunk rates higher than business principles on the political curb. The Brookharts are exalted above the Morrows. Seniority is a more valuable asset than all his dollars—and all his sense.

Politically, he is a misfit. He dislikes the men and the mechanics of our great national circus. Saved from equal disaster only by a remarkable intuitive sense, he almost matches Herbert Hoover in his ignorance of political etiquette and party fundamentals.

The slow and shoddy processes of the Senate, of democracy even, irritate him. He is not equipped to make a brave or boisterous showing in the Congressional chamber, yet that way lies success.

He is a man of thought rather than a leader, a curious and contemplative fellow rather than a doer, and that sort rarely succeeds in practical politics. Witness the records of William Howard Taft —a most excellent judge—and of Mr. Hoover—an eminently skillful promoter.

Both, however, may be classed as failures in the presidency.

Mr. Morrow is brainy but brittle, sagacious but slow. The same qualities which enabled him to attract more money to Morgan coffers than any single associate, and to act as the firm's brisk little buffer and diplomat, handicap him now.

As he was a conference-chamber lawyer and financier, so he is a committee-room Senator, and no more inspiring than such senatorial drudges as Reed Smoot of Utah and Wesley Jones of Washington.

A useful man but unemotional and unexcitable—as solid but as unattractive, politically, as a safety deposit box.

The Senate does not furnish a friendly environment for him. Used to that deference which his financial prominence gave him, he contends now with men who regard the money power as a basic, national evil. The "sons of the wild jackasses" only await a chance to haze this little son of the rich, and he dreads the encounter. He will learn, as has even the great Borah, that wisdom avails not against the wit of the waspish Caraway or the wisecracks of the irrepressible Pat Harrison.

He senses this latent and loutish antagonism, and he shrinks from it. He has looked on while his millionaire friends—"Dave" Reed of Pennsylvania and Hiram Bingham of Connecticut—were made to look ridiculous, notwithstanding their solemnity, by a hillbilly but hilarious Democrat from below the Mason and Dixon line. Thus it was that during his first session he sat, silent and birdlike, on the edge of his chair as a simple spectator.

Although a bigger and better man than recent Republican Presidents, both culturally and intellectually, he is too backward and bashful to make a deep or immediate imprint upon a capricious public. He cannot display flashy stuff on the floor, on the stump or on the front page. Therein lies the chief obstacle to his preferment.

He is unimpressive and unspectacular. So far he is only a famous name, and the voters grow weary of Republicans who come bearing naught but myths.

Three in a decade are plenty!

He is as vulnerable a candidate as the G.O.P. can advance. He is not, personally or politically, the man for the nation's present mood, which is restive and resentful at the shabby leadership shown by his present colleagues and his financial friends in "the street."

It is true that he is represented as out of sympathy with the narrow tenets of Hoover Republicanism. He is pictured as a man of progressive ideas and social vision. He must not be judged, we are told, by his years of servitude to Mammon. He was then simply taking the world as he found it, and shaping himself for public service to be performed somehow and somewhere.

It is much the same propaganda that was broadcast anent Mr. Hoover when he was only an ambitious Cabinet member. It is another promise that the Republicans have raised up a new Messiah to supplant and shame the old, foolish prophets.

His record, however, belies these advance notices. Mr. Morrow is a regular, conservative, party and platform member of the G.O.P. All his sympathies are for preservation of the status quo. Not only does he believe in the existing order and ordinations; he worships them. He gave fifteen years to underwriting the system at home and abroad. It is too much to expect that, suddenly and sinfully, he will set out to wreck or even modify it.

He is not so insensible to modern influences as "Jim" Watson, who would rather be reactionary than right. He is, however, inclined to think that to be reactionary is to be right. With Mr. Watson it is a fixation, with Mr. Morrow it is a faith.

Since his first venture into politics as a Taft delegate in 1912, when Wall Street saw Theodore

THE MIRRORS OF 1932

Roosevelt's mildly progressive movement as one of our first "red" menaces, he has exhibited no trace of economic or political liberalism.

What his friends mean, apparently, when they speak of his social conscience is the normal desire for decency which any person of intelligence entertains. This spirit he showed when he entered into a civic movement to "clean up" his home town of Englewood, and in sponsoring reformation of New Jersey's mediaeval prison system.

For the moment, the shadow of his Wall Street career darkens his path and thoughts.

Though the public may, he cannot forget that he was once a Morgan partner. Wall Street, which made him, now unmans him.

He has an excellent historical background, and he remembers that the House of Morgan, except for those gold-rush years of the Coolidge Administration, has been the bugaboo of American politics. He is, I suspect, one of the few members of the firm to be honored with high public office, if not the first, and he slid in on a golden platter.

He dare not be himself. He strives so studiedly to live down his immediate past that he has not yet got around to being a Senator. He has made no move to sustain the faltering legend that he is a naïve, likable, studious and statesmanlike figure about to burst across the political heavens with all the glamour of Son-in-Law and Vote-Getter Lindbergh.

If not ashamed of his past—which I doubt—he is seemingly afraid of the political ghosts imminent in it.

He is discovering that it is still easier for a camel to pass through the eye of a needle than for a Morgan partner to enter, unabashed and unreservedly, into the kingdom of politics. He exhibits this sense of uneasiness in his conversation and in his conduct in the Senate.

During his first session he declined to deliver speeches, to grant interviews, to take part in senatorial doings. He preferred to look and learn before he leaped, but he also feared lest he be deemed a presumptuous plutocrat turned politician. He would accept no assignment on important committees lest it be said that he was cashing in on finance and friendship. He rejected the suggestion that he go on the Banking and Currency Committee lest it be thought that Wall Street were packing that legislative agency.

His decision to shun such demagogic criticism has not been weakened by the fall of our financiers from grace. Times have changed since Calvin Coolidge godfathered him into politics as Ambassador to Mexico. The policies, the very philosophy, of the Coolidge-Morrow breed of men are under suspicion. He is, perhaps, wise in his silences.

From Mr. Morrow, through the period of unsound speculation, came no warning such as Paul Warburg voiced against presidential and governmental policies which permitted and aggravated the stock market crash. Although no man was closer to Mr. Coolidge than Classmate Morrow, the latter, apparently, withheld advice from his campus chum.

Mr. Morrow was, it would appear, as silent and undiscerning as Calvin was vocal. The lack of a wise and well-timed word from the great financier as he saw his good friend plunge the nation further into disaster is explainable only on the theory that Mr. Morrow was as blind as his brethren among the bulls and bears.

For his amazing senatorial reticence the Senator gives more personal reasons than those I have suggested. To his friends who beg him to show his stuff, and to editors who offer their columns, he replies:

"No, thank you! I have had enough publicity to last me the rest of my lifetime."

With which it is quite possible to agree. He has

been eulogized as the ablest diplomat of modern times, as a presidential candidate and as the Father-in-Law of Lindbergh. In fact, disgruntled dry spokesmen attributed his New Jersey triumph to the aviator-son rather than to the distinguished statesman. Though there was great guffawing at this explanation, the Honorable Franklin Fort, Mr. Morrow's opponent, discovered that Son-in-Law Lindbergh was his real conqueror.

Mr. Fort adduces convincing evidence. Toward the end of the primary he heard that two fanatically dry spinsters intended to vote for his wet opponent. When Mr. Fort, in order to satisfy himself of the existence of such sentiment, checked up, he was told that, despite their dryness and old friendship for him, they felt that they must vote for Mr. Morrow—

"Because he is the father of Lindbergh!"

Flyer and Financier, Son-in-Law and Father-in-Law, they made an unbeatable combination. Many thousands were influenced by the drama of the spectacle, and these, with wet Democrats, sent Mr. Morrow to the Senate. Ironically enough, the Senator did his utmost to keep Lindbergh out of the political picture, and he relegated the prohibition issue to the background.

He resents this sort of publicity, and he will not

capitalize it. He does not relish references to himself as "the Lindbergh of the Senate"—a phrase often used to satirize his silences and his air of inaccessibility.

Although seriously mentioned for the presidency, he turns upon his ballyhooers a pair of eyes as hard and cold as they can be friendly and sympathetic. He insists, with seeming sincerity, that he wants no such honor. He has been in all things deferential to Mr. Hoover.

Mr. Morrow, for example, would not consent to run for the Senate until he was assured that his candidacy would be satisfactory to the President. Subsequently, under some prodding from presidential emissaries, he announced that he hoped and expected to vote for Mr. Hoover again. Privately he advances an argument against his candidacy that may come nearer the truth.

"I have known three Presidents intimately," he says, "and I do not care to go through what they did."

The three are Woodrow Wilson, Mr. Coolidge and Mr. Hoover. He knew Mr. Wilson well through his war services and Princetonian connections; he was Mr. Coolidge's "Colonel House"; and, as a professional financier and amateur politician, he has enjoyed peculiar advantages for observing the mess Mr. Hoover has made of things.

The Senator has little in common with the President. Mr. Morrow has a profound rather than a political conviction on prohibition, and he can hardly approve the Chief Executive's handling of this great question. Mr. Morrow believes in direct dealing with problems and people, especially in the field of practical affairs, and he does not sympathize with government by commissions.

The President, on his side, is extremely jealous of the diminutive Napoleon of finance, all the more so because Wall Street and its operations are a meaningless morass to him. Did not Mr. Hoover, when the financial crash came, solemnly announce that the panic would be confined within the limits of Trinity churchyard and the East River!

Mr. Hoover becomes alarmed at hints that he step aside in favor of this Senate fledgling.

In his relations with Mr. Morrow the man in the White House has shown some shrewdness. He has courted the Senator almost shamelessly. He has, it seems, tried to place the financier under such deep obligations that he cannot repudiate them by permitting even fanciful mention of himself as a presidential candidate.

THE MIRRORS OF 1932

Mr. Hoover sent Mr. Morrow to London as a naval delegate. Upon the morning of the delegation's return Mr. Hoover insisted upon an immediate conference with the man then mentioned as his possible successor, and, though no understanding was reached, the atmosphere was so friendly that it caused chagrin in the Morrow-for-President camp. Subsequently, Mr. Hoover gave a formal indorsement of the Morrow senatorial campaign at the very moment when he was refusing to extend a helping hand to drys seeking reelection on a platform of "Stand by the President."

By his cry of "Kamerad" Mr. Hoover may have directed the Senator's thoughts toward the vice-presidency instead of the White House itself. But it has not prevented influential interests in the party from keeping the Senator in mind as an alternative candidate.

If the financial and political boys could dictate the ticket, and if it were not so difficult to dislodge the Commander-in-Chief of the Republican Army, Mr. Morrow would be almost a first-ballot choice over Mr. Hoover.

Very real considerations move the groups which prefer Mr. Morrow to Mr. Hoover as the 1932 standard-bearer. The politicians, many of them

DWIGHT WHITNEY MORROW

facing defeat as a result of Administration failures, think the Senator's name would restore confidence in the Republican Party as the ark of prosperity. The financiers think that, with him in the White House, there would be more sanity and steadiness at the top.

These elements, whose politics and profit it is to know their candidates, have no doubt that Mr. Morrow would be safe and sound—just another Republican President. These men have no objection to a social vision and conscience which content themselves with wiping out vicious conditions in a New Jersey hamlet or jail.

They need only to examine Mr. Morrow's senatorial record to discover that his attitude on the graver problems of society and government are eminently correct. By the same sign, those who envisage him as a blushing Progressive, with large or small "p," may come upon disillusionment, as they have with respect to Mr. Hoover.

Mr. Morrow voted for confirmation of appointments to the Federal Power and Tariff Commissions which were, to say the least, questionable and worthy of more serious scrutiny than the Senate majority gave. He opposed all proposals for public operation of Muscle Shoals, or for distribution of

THE MIRRORS OF 1932

electrical energy to surrounding municipalities and States on an equitable basis.

He refused to furnish more generous relief for unemployed and drought sufferers than Mr. Hoover and the Red Cross would permit. He even opposed Senator Capper's innocent plan under which the Federal Farm Board would have turned over 20,000,000 bushels of rotting wheat to the hungry.

He lined up as a "big navy" Senator even when the modernization measures he supported required appropriations which would have relieved a great deal of distress. He felt so strongly against liberalizing the loan provisions of the bonus act that he was, strangely, tempted, but only tempted, to deliver an oration.

Except on prohibition matters he was as typical a time-server as any standpatter from backward and backboneless regions. He voted to lift the limitations on physicians' liquor prescriptions, and against an enforcement measure for the beliquored Capital that was a legislative abortion.

His record disposes, most effectively, of the suggestion that he may be the apostle of a new day and a new deal in the Republican Party. It qualifies him, not as Mr. Hoover's rival, but as the latter's running mate.

As a presidential candidate—or even as a seeker after second honors—those Morgan memories would haunt and hurt him. There is scarcely a provocative issue of American politics on which, first as Morgan lawyer and subsequently as trouble man, he has not become involved. He was, to be sure, acting under a private rather than a public code, but the voters can hardly be trusted to draw such a fine distinction.

Morgan money has financed armaments in Europe, including the castor-oil régime of Benito Mussolini, and sugar in a Cuba controlled by methods none too democratic. It has created a vast structure of public utilities—railroads, street railways, lighting and heating systems and hydroelectric plants. Only the year before Mr. Morrow joined the firm, the late George F. Baker testified in the "money trust" investigation—which was sponsored, oddly enough, by the bolshevistic sire of Son-in-Law Lindbergh—that no great enterprise could succeed without the approval of himself or Morgan.

Yet Mr. Morrow was a salutary influence at

Broad and Wall Streets. With a canny consideration for the value of good will, he transformed the ruthless and frigid atmosphere there into one suavely sweet and sensible. It is now more informally run than the Senate, or it was when he quit.

Many a time the New Jersey member kept the directors waiting while he argued faculty problems with a visiting professor or fellow-trustee of his Alma Mater. "J.P." might growl and rage, but his young partner chatted on and on about "the college on the hill," his legs curled under him. Twice—once when he was offered the presidency of Amherst College and again when Yale University tried to get him as it head—his partners almost resorted to force to prevent him from burying himself beneath campus elms and ivy.

Morgan needed Mr. Morrow far more than Mr. Morrow needed Morgan. The Senator calmed many a storm which might have shaken "the street." He brought a new and fine spirit into the firm even in handling the first important legal matter entrusted to him—the defense of the firm's financing of the bankrupt New Haven railroad.

Whereas hard-boiled legalists of an older generation had stubbornly, and foolishly, contested the Interstate Commerce Commission's first investiga-

DWIGHT WHITNEY MORROW

tion, withholding records and quarrelling over every detail, Mr. Morrow gave full cooperation to the federal agency in the second inquiry, and was honorably mentioned in the commission's final report, even though Morgan and his New Haven puppets were not.

Nevertheless, the means by which Mr. Morrow cleansed the Morgan stables hardly makes the stuff of which sympathetic campaign speeches are built.

If he was a new type of big banker, he was also a refreshing figure in the field of diplomacy. In conciliation he shines. As nature abhors a vacuum, so he dislikes disagreements over policies or personalities, even though he may not be directly involved.

"He cannot see two men at odds," says Senator "Dave" Reed, "without letting his mind play, immediately and instinctively, on ways and means of bringing them together. He is a born diplomat."

Although he has already exhibited this trait behind the scenes of the Senate, his most dramatic demonstration was at Mexico City. The two nations were drifting toward armed conflict when Mr. Morrow suggested to Friend Calvin that he be permitted to try his talents. So he supplanted Ambassador Sheffield, who had counted that day lost in which he did not notify our State Department of the wickedness and unregeneracy of Mexico and Mexicans.

"Personnel rather than formulas make for success," the new Ambassador once gave as his prescription for difficulties such as he faced in his new post, and he was now the "personnel."

He sent no long letters to our State Department. To all practical purposes, he was President, Secretary of State and Ambassador.

His first act was to hire a taxicab, motor around to the palace and meet President Calles. He drove about the countryside with Calles for many days, trying to establish friendly terms, before mentioning the troublesome issue of confiscated oil lands. He discussed and arbitrated the most serious disputes through the Mexican government's own interpreter. He called in a prominent Roman Catholic to aid in compromising the differences between the Church and State.

He got a complete and sympathetic understanding of Mexico—its racial, social, economic, industrial and political history—by constant study and the employment of a research staff. He paid with his own funds for the services of George Rublee, the foremost expert on Mexican matters. He walked through the market place, he visited honored shrines, he sat reading *Don Quixote* in the parks. He might have been a stubby, swarthy Mexican himself.

He flattered these courtly but childlike Latins, maintaining a fleet of motor cars and a fine cellar of rare wines. He entertained lavishly but democratically. He made of his assignment a holiday. Between conferences he passed the life of the Latin that he is. He read, lounged about his country estate, watched flowers grow and sunsets die.

"Meesa Morrow," gibbered his gardener in describing one of the Ambassador's rare mornings, "shake hands with me one, two t'ree times. He come into the garden t'ree times just for that. And for why he shake hands with Sancho t'ree times? Because the sun is shining!"

And when "Meesa Morrow" sailed for London, he bethought himself halfway across that his charge d'affaires was a comparatively poor man. So he cabled credit of $60,000 that the ambassadorial menage might be maintained in the style to which the Mexicans had become accustomed.

If all public life consisted of dealing with such people and such problems, Mr. Morrow might achieve that fanciful freedom of spirit which he seeks.

Our Senators—alas!—are neither childlike nor courtly, as he has so soon discovered. Nor is he a practical or practicing politician.

He detests the details and he will not learn them. He seeks escape from sordid contact with his humble henchmen; he flees from the barest political duties of his office.

As late as the eve of his entry into politics, he did not know the names of the State leaders. He declined to dictate the platform even though everybody deferred to his wishes and wisdom. He turns all patronage over to his colleague, "Ham" Kean. This sort of responsibility he will not accept, and it may yet prove to be the flaw in his armor.

When the politicians seek him out, for advice or more material support, he is apt to be in conference at 10 Downing Street or the Quai d'Orsay rather than with the home-town boys in their humble district clubs at Jersey City, Newark and Trenton. He is a bad political guesser, as he showed in advocating the League of Nations in 1920.

He got along surprisingly well with the gang in his campaign, however. From Mr. Coolidge he got the sound advice of "Let the other feller do the talkin'," and he ignored his opponent more devastatingly than Mr. Hoover ignored Alfred E. Smith. He went where the bosses sent him, and he did what they told him.

In one respect he disappointed the politicians most grievously. They hung around in vain for his money bags to open. Although reckless of personal expenditures, he was religiously scrupulous of political spending. He was obsessed with the fear that he might be charged with having purchased his seat, and he named as campaign manager the son of a Scotch brick mason.

All New Jersey, it seemed, turned out to stare at the great financier who had come seeking their suffrage. The people knew not whether to be delighted or disillusioned. What they saw was a short and stubby fellow whose shambling manner was that of a shy and scared man.

The males suffered no inferiority complex—and that was to his advantage—as they noted his unassuming and unaffected bearing, his rumpled hair and his uncreased suits. The women wanted to mother the boyish figure who was, obviously, so hesitant and awkward.

Whereas they had counted on a spectacular show, he awakened no awe or emotion. He did not stir or startle them. But he spoke in terrific earnest, and he had horse sense—a rare quality in New Jersey's recent senatorial candidates. So they trusted him and voted for him.

About his camp, however, hung an air of awful amiability. He took counsel only with himself on important questions, and, once he had made up his stubborn mind, he could not be moved. His relations with the press were unfortunate, for he clung to the earlier Morgan and Lindbergh tradition of reserve and silence. He was always polite, but always detached and disinterested.

"No, thank you," then as now, expressed his state of mind.

Mr. Morrow is represented as an extremely simple and democratic fellow.

He may be. He is friendly and affable, he prefers his pants unpressed, he cannot comb his unruly hair, he looks more like a brick-layer than a banker. He revels in bees, roses and sunlight, he reads ancient history and semi-religious works, he plays a good game of golf and bridge, he strews cigarettes about his luxurious home with abandon, he refers to the evening meal as "supper" and rarely dresses for it. It is true, too, that he puts on no side.

DWIGHT WHITNEY MORROW

These, however, are hardly the true Jeffersonian qualities; they are but the Tolstoyan externals of democracy

He can be, and often is, cold, brusque, dictatorial. He is inaccessible, not physically but spiritually. He confides in only a few, and those he must know well. His invariable answer to correspondents at the Capital, who are rapidly conceiving a strong dislike for him, is "I do not care to be interviewed."

With the world he is snobbish and standoffish, not in a personal but in a philosophic sense. His famed absent-mindedness is a fortification rather than forgetfulness.

The secret of his abstractions—about which legend already rises—is that ordinary people and ordinary affairs do not interest him. His absent-mindedness is simply deliberate concentration on thoughts far from the immediate chatter and circumstances. He grasps things quickly, and, having absorbed so much as he desires or requires, he thereupon withdraws into a consciousness of inner or distant things.

His mind moves like his strangely stubby legs—in quick jerks.

THE MIRRORS OF 1932

There is as much pragmatism as romanticism in his makeup. He is, perhaps, the most baffling figure at the Capital.

Two anecdotes furnish some clew to the conflicting chapters of his career and character.

The first is told by his friends. They relate how Mr. Morrow, while travelling on a train one late afternoon, could not find his railroad ticket. As he fussed and searched for it in vain, the conductor explained that, of course, the great Mr. Morrow could ride without producing legal proof that he had paid his fare.

"But," sputtered the banker-diplomat-statesman, "if I don't find my ticket, I won't know where I'm supposed to deliver a speech to-night."

Mr. Morrow tells a different, and a more likely tale. It was, according to his version, a Scotchman who was unable to find his ticket. When it was subsequently discovered between his lips, his friends subjected him to some ridicule for such droll absent-mindedness. To which the victim replied:

"You domn fools—I was sucking off the date."

JOSEPH TAYLOR ROBINSON

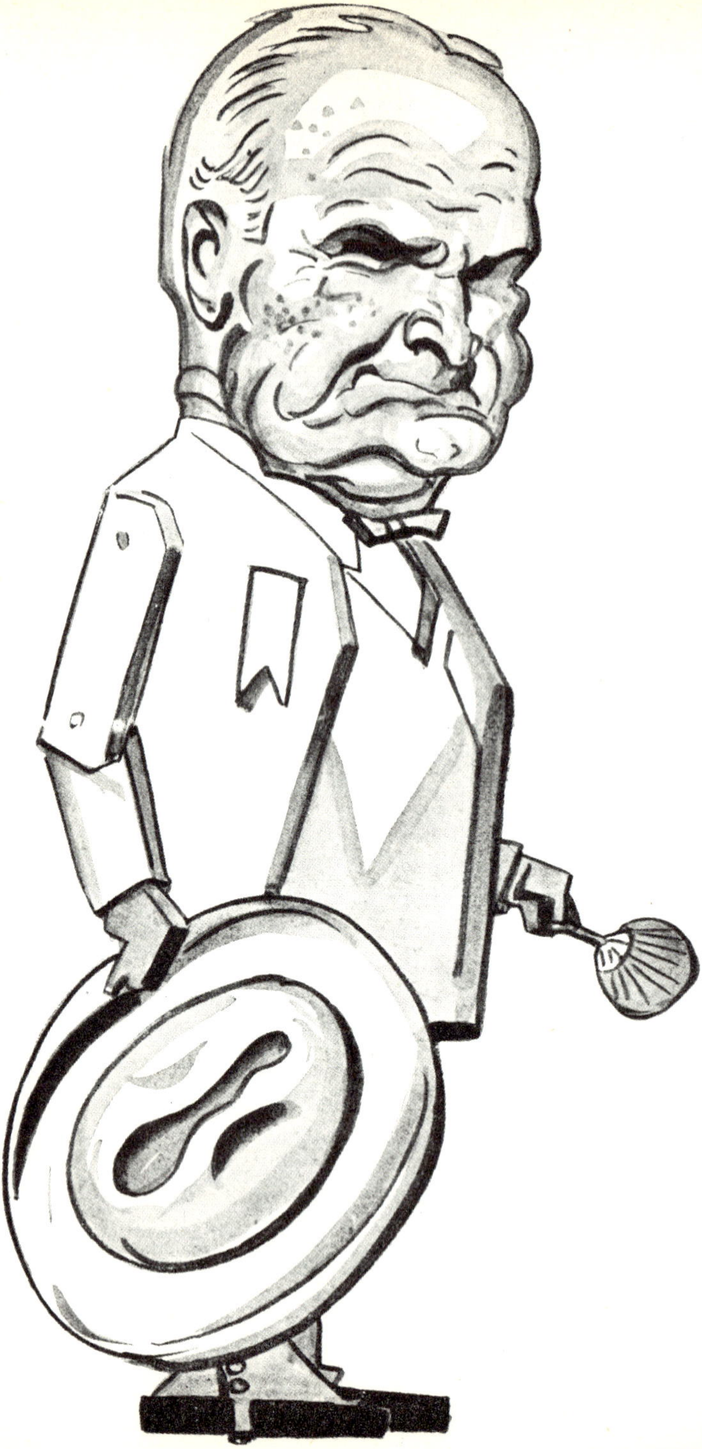

SENATOR JOSEPH T. ROBINSON

Joe Robinson, like most southerners who serve in the United States Senate a while, has succumbed to the temptations of a devilishly clever, conservative, Republican Capital.

The plainsman from Arkansas, who entered the House of Representatives as an humble, homespun, hill-billy Democrat almost thirty years ago, has become a political plutocrat.

Although it is a fate which befalls most statesmen from below the Mason and Dixon line, Mr. Robinson happens to be its prize victim and exhibit. Although the outcome exposes the workings of the system, it also shows up Joe.

It may not be too late for the sinning Squire from Arkansas to repent, provided knowledge and strength are given unto him. In any event, his story may save others from the same pitfalls.

Except that he fell farther, Joe can scarcely be blamed for slipping. There have been scores before him. One by one, as novel attractions and associations dull their memory of Jeffersonian simplicity and Democratic doctrine, these simple southerners seek to escape from the grub to the butterfly state.

After a few years in Washington they begin to be ashamed of the personal crudities and parochial loyalties which have set them apart. They forget and forswear the things their ancestors bled for and for which they shed tears and oratory on the home hustings each Fourth of July.

Even "The War Between the States" becomes, on their lips, "The Civil War."

Power, place, prestige appear both desirable and possible of attainment. They begin to crave, no less, political respectability. They would rather eat, drink and be merry than carry on the old faith and fight.

Personal popularity becomes preferable to political exile in a crowded and charming city. They long for friendly headlines in Washington's bitterly partisan newspapers; for R.S.V.P.'s instead of rebuffs; invitations to White House and Cabinet dinners; association with the great and the gay.

Their political principles undergo the same softening and transformation.

SENATOR JOSEPH T. ROBINSON

After all, it's hard to break sweetbreads with Andrew W. Mellon of a late evening and then denounce his official ethics next day on the Senate floor. It's not pleasant to wash down White House mutton with a fillip at Herbert Hoover's political philosophy.

Moreover, these Republican magnificos—and magnificats—are difficult to resist. Lords and ladies, they are really splendid people in evening dress. As Eleanor Patterson, the former Countess Gyzicki, says of Alice Longworth, "she can burn you up with personality when she cares to."

"Dave" Reed can be the most charming companion imaginable, as Mr. Robinson discovered when the two served together at the London Naval Conference.

Even Henry L. Stimson and Charles F. Adams—those stiff Cabinet curios—unbent across the seas, far from this prohibition province, and Mr. Robinson found them to be most gracious.

It is, in fact, a great life. But the Robinsons, unfortunately, weaken. They soon get worldly wisdom and philosophize thus:

"It's a pretty good world. Live and let live. The country won't suffer much, no matter which party's in power. Let's see, where do we eat to-night—with the Jimmie Curtis's or the Ambassador of Siam?"

That, without much exaggeration, is the story of Joe Robinson. Its more recent chapter might well be entitled The Great Seduction.

It explains why there has been no aggressive minority on Capitol Hill since he became Democratic leader in 1922. It explains why the only thing which divides the two parties in the Senate is a four-foot aisle.

It explains why sneers and snarls are the portion which many of his colleagues mete to him. Said one Democrat in an aside—for Joe's great bulk, beetling brows and bull-like voice affright the rebellious—as the latter plodded through the Senate anteroom:

"There, by the grace of a trip to London, walks Sir Herbert Hoover's Prime Minister."

Even to close friends Joe has become a pain and a puzzle. For years a seemingly solid, sensible, friendly soul, he has become a mad bull in a Democratic china closet, and, by the same sign, a joy and comfort to the Republicans. As Al Smith said, "He has given more aid to Herbert Hoover than any other Democrat."

On the attack he has faltered and in defense he

SENATOR JOSEPH T. ROBINSON

has been feeble. Again and again he leads his forces against his good friend in the White House, only to supplicate or surrender at the critical moment. He marches Senate Democrats up the hill and down again until they grow faint and footsore. He is abject and apologetic even in the flush of triumph.

His judgment, over almost a decade, has been faulty and unfortunate. In the Coolidgean era, when people refused to become wrought up over partisan disputes, he thundered and bellowed against the harmless Calvin. He hurled political pinpricks against a White House of solid gold. But when the depression gave the outs the finest opportunity since Taft's last years, he formed an alliance with the despised and waning party in power.

More than any other individual, perhaps, he is responsible for the belief that there is no difference between the two major parties. When the people cry "A plague on both your houses!" they are thinking, even though unconsciously, of the joint efforts of Damon Robinson and Pythias Hoover.

Oddly, the Senator has done his most heroic battling against his own associates. It is he who has provoked dissension among Democrats over prohibition on the eve of a presidential campaign in which they hope for victory. Consciously or unconsciously, he is playing straight into Mr. Hoover's hands—again.

If this issue again divides his party, it will be due, chiefly, to the violence he displays in discussing it. His spectacular outbreak at the winter conference of the National Committee in 1931 was an unforgettable scene.

As ever, it was not so much what he said as how he said it. His attack, characteristically, was apoplectic. It consisted of incoherent and intemperate bravado and blustering, heightened by a reddened and maniacal visage, rolling eyes, revolving arms, stamping feet. Joe always mistakes fury for force and energy for emphasis. He forgets himself upon such oratorical occasions, and he is borne beyond himself by his own sound waves.

Although the Senator's speech made him the holy hero—and, mayhap, martyr—of the drys, it made him a little ridiculous in the eyes of all neutral men. It was clear to all that he had simply grabbed at the chance to create an impression on the assembled committeemen.

His excitability would have evoked at least sympathy had he, in the past, proved himself a pro-

SENATOR JOSEPH T. ROBINSON

hibitionist through conviction rather than expediency. But his record on that subject hardly warrants such a view.

The White Ribboners swarmed into Arkansas when he ran for Governor in 1912, raising insistent cries that local option be supplanted by a bone-dry statute. Although Joe had the support of the distillers' lobbyists, he promised to sign a prohibition bill if the Legislature passed one, and he kept the pledge.

In the Senate he voted to submit the Eighteenth Amendment to the States for ratification. But partisanship eventually got the better of his prohibition zeal, and he voted to sustain Woodrow Wilson's veto of the Volstead Act.

In 1928 he made no murmur when Al Smith repudiated the Houston convention's dry plank and hoisted the flag of repeal. Joe's nomination, as he must have known, was a deliberate straddle. He was named solely as a sop to the Bible Belt and the Anti-Saloon League cohorts. But he was quite happy to fill this role and he concealed his qualms, if he had any, at Al's backsliding.

So snickers were considered quite parliamentary when he warned Al and Johnnie Raskob that "You cannot substitute the skull and bones of an outlawed trade as the banner of the Democratic party."

There is no mystery in the Senator's strange behaviour, however, much as it may perplex his partisans. He suffers from growing pains, albeit he is sixty years old.

These have been aggravated by odd conceits which, since his vice-presidential venture, have quite undermined his wonted good nature and good sense. He is no longer the big, overgrown boy from the sticks who once boasted more friends on both sides of the aisle than any other Senator. He is no more the intense Democrat whom Wilson, out of gratitude for Joe's ready worship of the War President, dubbed "the moral and intellectual leader of the Senate."

Joe, in short, feels the bite of the presidential bee in every part of his expansive anatomy, probably because he has withheld no portion of his broad area from the insidious insect. The first southerner to be named even for second place since 1861, he is pleased to envisage himself as the first to be nominated for the Presidency itself.

Everybody except himself deems the idea grand but preposterous, especially in the light of his de-

SENATOR JOSEPH T. ROBINSON

sertion and downfall, but that simply fires him with a more morose ambition. It is a fixation. He is, he feels, One against the World. Mad from goadings and jibings, he is the Lear of national politics.

Yet it was not, as so many think, his taste of high life in London that spoiled the Squire from Lonoke County, Ark. That simply completed the job.

Long ago he revealed the range of his acrobatic ambition when he leaped from the House of Representatives to the Governorship and to the Senate within two months.

It is a political span accomplished by no other man in public life. He doubtless and deservingly cherishes the honor. Nevertheless, it discloses those fatal qualities of opportunism and self-seeking which have only lately shown themselves in such sharp and sorrowful shape.

Elected Governor at a crucial period in American history—1912—and on a platform embodying numerous State reforms, he forgot his pledges when a vacancy appeared in the Senate. Figuratively at least, even as he delivered his inaugural address, he kept one eye on the timetable of trains to the Capital. He got the Legislature to send him back to the Congress he had left, but to the silk-stockinged branch.

London did affect him, however. There he learned how the better half lives. He dined and slept in the palaces of kings and queens. He hobnobbed with royalty, both British and American, and dressed for dinner. He talked their language—or tried to—and it is to be expected that he assimilated some of their ideas.

For months he was the buddy of such splendid Democrats as Senator Reed, Dwight W. Morrow, Secretary Adams, Secretary Stimson and Ambassador Dawes. His closest and most congenial chums, as subsequent events in the Senate were to show, were those two sturdy sansculottes—Messrs. Reed and Morrow.

He consorted with intellectuals and he caught glimpses of a rarefied universe. This half-starved countryman from the lowly and backward State of Arkansas was strangely stirred by these encounters. He chatted plain with George Bernard Shaw and Gilbert K. Chesterton at Nancy Astor's week-end parties.

He became Nancy's favorite house guest. The Virginia Langhorne, perhaps out of a fellow feeling for another political expatriate, took a liking to this drawling, homespun, muscular frontiersman.

Strangely, in view of what the British—and Mr.

SENATOR JOSEPH T. ROBINSON

Hoover—did to him, Nancy was especially taken by his seemingly robust, Democratic spirit. In chaffing response to his presentation of American friends, she would toss back her head and inquire: "But are you sure he's a Democrat, Joe?"

The question seems ironic to his colleagues, who suspect that he is no longer an authority on Democrats or democracy. Did he not return from London and such nonsensical goings-on, they ask, a subdued man? Did he not, quite ostentatiously, let his legs protrude into Senate aisles to exhibit a new pair of bright, grey spats?

In retrospect, his associates recall that he was always given to putting on side, though of an innocent nature. In the Congressional Directory, for instance, he lists himself as a graduate of historic University of Virginia, although he simply attended summer school there. Whether through shame or neglect, he forgets to mention in the same biographical sketch that he was Al Smith's running mate, and disastrously defeated.

So it is not surprising that his sojourn at St. James's Palace changed him. Of late years he has been subjected to temptations which befall few Democrats of any breed. It was, too, his misfortune that they were showered upon him quite suddenly, and at a time when age, ambition and associations combined to make him peculiarly susceptible.

For years he has led an extremely modest and retiring life. An office-holder since he was twenty-four years old, he has had few advantages. Arkansas is not noted for its social or intellectual pursuits. Mr. Robinson himself, during the drought relief controversy, made it out to be the "Orphan Annie" of the forty-eight States. His fellow-Senator, Thaddeus H. Caraway, deepened this impression with his amazing confession that his own brother had no pants good enough to wear to a House of God on Sabbath Day.

Joe, in short, was a sort of indigenous innocent abroad.

In Little Rock he occupies a modest $14,000 home. His circle, even though it numbers Harvey Couch, influential power magnate and friend of Mr. Hoover, is narrow. At Washington the Senator has an apartment in the building which houses the Methodist Board of Temperance, Prohibition and Public Morals—the so-called Methodist Vatican—where occupants are not even permitted to smoke.

Thus, for the youngster who progressed from a

SENATOR JOSEPH T. ROBINSON

rural family of ten children to the United States Senate, his stay in London marked a new, if not a Democratic, day. So, in any event, think his colleagues.

From the first they warned against his going. They sensed that it would tie him too closely to the Administration and devitalize his powers of leadership.

"He'll come back a mouthpiece instead of a spokesman," prophesied Mr. Caraway with uncanny foresight.

Joe, however, wanted his fling, and he sought the appointment by every proper means. The Administration, of course, sent him along solely as Democratic ballast. Mr. Hoover did not mean to repeat the mistake committed by Mr. Wilson when the latter let none but Democrats go to Versailles.

They gave Joe little to do at London. Mr. Stimson handled all negotiations with the British, Mr. Reed with the Japanese, Mr. Morrow with the French and Italians, who must borrow their funds from J. P. Morgan & Co.

Joe sat around in his best togs, window-shopped in Piccadilly—and advised solemnly. His sole act of importance was a disservice to Secretary Stimson. It was the Senator who informed American correspondents that the United States, in its desire to reduce armaments, had insisted on the right to construct a super-dreadnaught. Mr. Stimson, furious at the disclosure, does not know to this day who gave out this bad news.

Joe's complete seduction became evident even before his return to this country. He was still in London, fighting for Mr. Hoover, when Democrats and Progressives opened sharp fire on the nomination of Charles Evans Hughes to be Chief Justice of the Supreme Court. For a few days only a handful of Senators questioned Mr. Hughes's fitness to return to the bench, and the incident seemed likely to pass off quietly.

As the conflict continued, however, conservative Democrats from the South grew restless. They squirmed in their seats and heard the call of partisanship. They talked of joining the melee and providing the necessary votes to defeat confirmation. The leaderless southerners, at the close of a particularly turbulent skirmish, were about to give this turn to the struggle.

The consequences would have been historic. Had they lined up against Mr. Hughes, he might have been kept off the bench. It would have been the severest rebuke to a President since Andrew Jackson's day.

SENATOR JOSEPH T. ROBINSON

But Mr. Hoover bethought himself of his good friend across the water. There was an emergency message by cable or transatlantic telephone, and a hurried reply. Joe let his confidential spokesmen know that he opposed any action which might be interpreted as playing politics with the Supreme Court. Thus he calmed the restive Democrats and held them in leash for Mr. Hoover. Moreover, when the roll was called, the absent leader—some called him "the lost leader"—paired in favor of the nominee.

Robinson, I understand, rued his precipitate action upon his return. He told a Progressive critic of Mr. Hughes that he had been "misinformed" by his Republican friends in this country, and that he would not have intervened had he known the true situation.

This deception, if such it was, did not deter him from serving as the President's spokesman during the debate on the naval pact. Although he had led the fight against the 1922 agreement, which actually restricted navies, he pleaded for ratification of the London document, notwithstanding that it permitted construction of the largest and most formidable armadas in history.

Democratic mutterings against the treaty were stilled by his attitude. He carried the day for Mr.

Hoover. He consummated what the President regards as his finest achievement in the field of foreign policy.

Joe's colleagues were again dismayed and downcast. Their predictions anent his reaction to his trip abroad had come true. But what they did not know was that Mr. Robinson, rightly or wrongly, nourished the notion that Mr. Hoover would name him to the Supreme Court. He thought that he would be chosen to fill the place withheld by the Senate from Judge John J. Parker of North Carolina. But Mr. Hoover, with characteristic gratitude, forgot Mr. Robinson's Democratic misdeeds, and gave the post to Owen J. Roberts, a Pennsylvania Republican.

It suggests some gullibility in Joe to discover that even this misunderstanding, and the "misrepresentation" in the Hughes affair, did not disturb his alliance with the White House. Nor did several differences with the President in the drought relief dispute wean Joe away, although they shattered his colleagues' faith in their leader's intelligence and independence.

The Senator was both a comic and a pathetic figure during this period. On one day he shed tears on the floor as he pictured starvation and suffering

SENATOR JOSEPH T. ROBINSON

in Arkansas. On another day, in anger at White House indifference, he pledged a Democratic caucus to a finish fight on behalf of more generous assistance to the hungry and the cold and the shelterless. On a third, without any warning to his embattled and enthusiastic mates, he accepted Mr. Hoover's "compromise," and turned against his own program.

Joe was, this time, seduced openly and shamelessly. What is more, he seemed to like it. Actually, Mr. Hoover had called in Mr. Couch, whose vast corporation interests are handled by Mr. Robinson's law firm, and the latter lost his belligerence, the Democrats their cause and captain.

For this betrayal, however, he was subjected to as rough a drubbing and tongue-slashing as any Senate leader has taken from his own party in recent political history. Joe seemed to concede that he deserved it. He slumped, small and shamefacedly, into his chair. He became so unnerved that he tried to light his cigar on the Senate floor.

The incident is typical of his more recent generalship. It reveals the principal reasons for his failures. Instead of accepting advice from his associates, or taking them into his confidence, he acted, as always, in an arbitrary and headstrong manner.

THE MIRRORS OF 1932

He made a major decision of policy, and then sought to browbeat them into line behind him.

There is a great deal of the bully in the Senator's methods. He possesses many of the qualities of the vanishing, old-fashioned type of political boss. He rules, chiefly, by his physical power, which he has in great degree. Although not the tallest, he is undoubtedly the most vigorous and formidable member of the Senate. He conveys the impression of brute, animal strength, and a willingness to use it.

He has a hot temper, somewhat mellowed by the years. As a youthful lawyer and a member of the House he won a reputation as a firebrand. Only a few years ago he was expelled from an exclusive golf club because he knocked down a prominent physician with a straight to the jaw.

A trivial argument over shooting through while a thrifty member of Joe's senatorial quartet—Thomas J. Walsh of Montana—searched for a lost ball resulted in words, and with Joe in those days words often led to blows. The Robinsons have always been two-fisted men. It is the Senator's boast that his Baptist-preacher sire, even when seventy years old, could hold his own at fisticuffs.

Joe is the Democrats' bad man still. He cows

SENATOR JOSEPH T. ROBINSON

his henchmen as did podestas of the jungle school of politics—Charles F. Murphy, Roger Sullivan, Bill Vare and Boies Penrose. I have heard Democratic Senators admit, ruefully, that a hard look or angry word from him instills fear in them. Moreover, he retaliates against recalcitrants by petty slights in the award of committee memberships and other choice plums.

Those subtler and finer qualities of leadership—intellectual superiority and personal charm—have been withheld from him. There are, indeed, half a dozen men on the Democratic side who possess greater force and penetration and originality, but their political youthfulness and indifference to advancement stand in their way. Tradition alone, if naught else, prevents the Democrats from unseating an elected leader. It would be a confession of failure they dare not make.

Mr. Robinson's keenest lack is purpose and originality. Senate Democrats, under him, have no definite program. They line up, now with the Progressives, now with the Republicans. They suffer from the mistakes of these chameleonlike coalitions, and profit nothing by their successes. They are, it appears, content to wag—and wail.

In eight years the Senator has marched them

around in circles which, whether he realizes it or not, have brought him and his band into Mr. Hoover's backyard.

Mr. Robinson's merry-go-round has found him and his men on all sides of almost every major question. He has never been able to control all of them on anything. Five are certain to furnish sufficient votes to give victory to the Republicans even on such an historic issue as the tariff. The same number, including Mr. Robinson himself on one notable occasion, reinforce the Republicans on the public utility issue. They split helter-skelter on prohibition.

Lacking originality, Joe develops most of his ideas and strategy on the floor—and on his feet. He holds no conferences, trusts no lieutenants, and consults only himself.

While his colleagues are still pondering how they shall vote on a measure or an impromptu proposal, Joe leaps to his feet to express his views of the moment. Thus, unthinkingly, he commits the party to a definite policy. Should he discover that he has not voiced the sentiment of the minority, or even his own considered thought, it is too late to shift. Nevertheless, he will shift under pressure, thereby drawing the indictment of vacillation or worse.

SENATOR JOSEPH T. ROBINSON

The popular impression that Mr. Robinson is a forceful figure and a decisive leader derives from his speeches, and his manner of speaking. Nobody can tear to tatters a passion—or a party—more ruthlessly than Joe.

His voice, tremendous, hard, metallic, carries almost to the other side of the Capitol Building. Effortlessly, it rises to a booming baritone, and there it remains pitched. He has never learned to master or moderate it. His speeches are constant flows of sound meant to be majestic.

He paces the Senate aisle or well like a pre-historic creature. He pounds every piece of government property within reach. His powerful arms rotate like windmills, his fists knotted, veined, doubled. His body rumbles and rolls. A low hissing punctuates his periods as he strives for wind *ad infinitum.*

In Arkansas he has a reputation as a great orator.

Off the Senate floor, apart from politics, Joe is a simple and cosy sort of fellow. His bluster then appears to be no more than western breeziness. People like his apparent naïveté and simplicity. He is an outdoor man—a man's man—the best duck shot on Capitol Hill, a more skillful fisherman than his friend, Mr. Hoover, and a delightful companion afield.

A good story teller and a conscientious listener, he then displays nothing of the bumptiousness which marks his political career.

He is one of Washington's most regular window-shoppers. After an evening at the movies, he walks home through the fashionable shopping district with his nose glued to the plate glass panes.

I would not be surprised if this weakness for window-shopping supplies the deepest insight into Joe's character. He has, too long, stood on the outside looking on and in. He would be done with window-shopping and gazing into the homes of the great and the gay.

He would, in short, sit there himself—if not in St. James's Palace, at least in the White House.

ALBERT C. RITCHIE

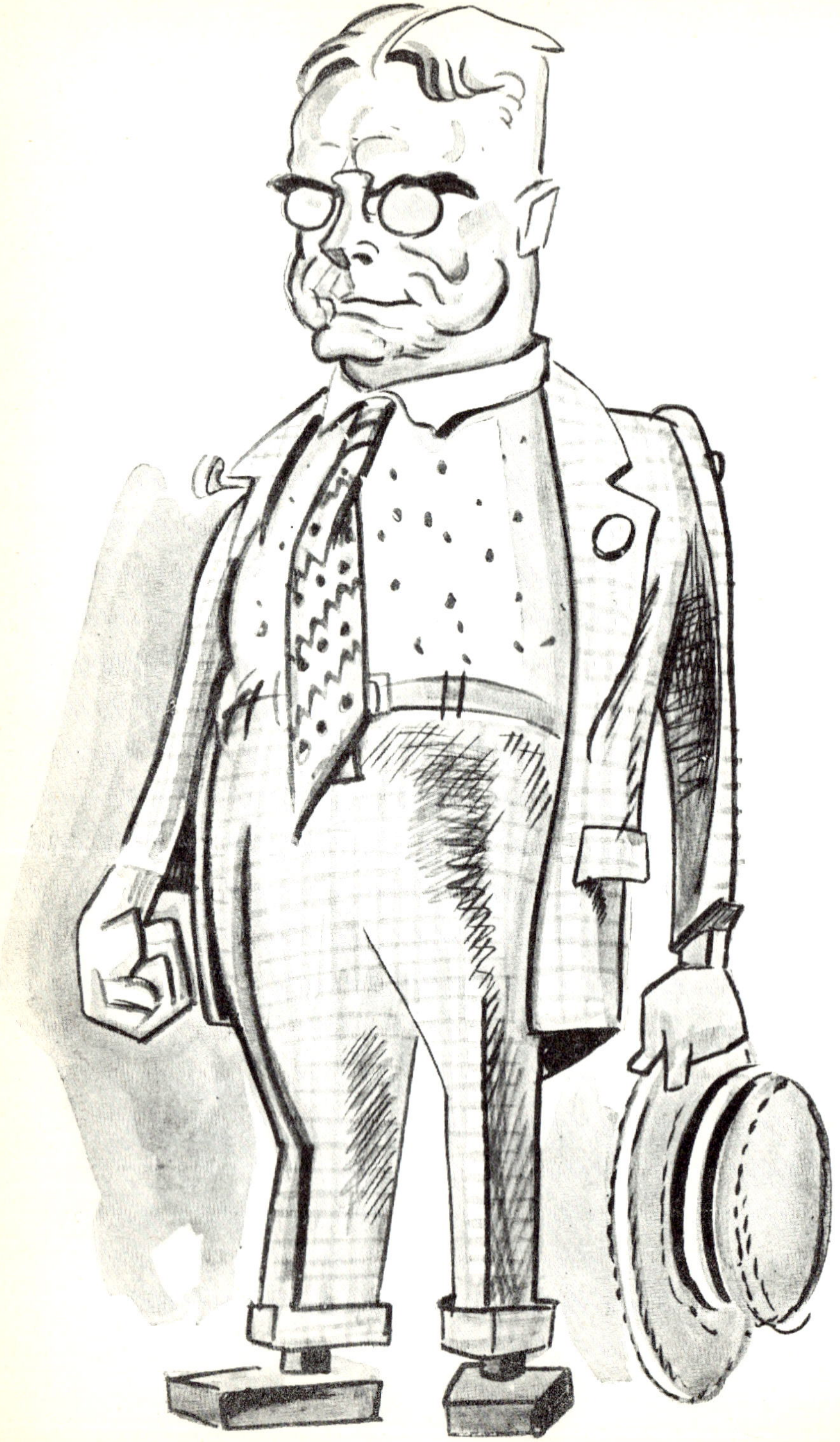

ALBERT C. RITCHIE

Albert Cabell Ritchie's bid for the presidency is based on sentiment rather than sense.

He has a cry but not a cause.

It is the dead doctrine of States' Rights.

Although his theory died at Appomattox, he tries desperately to infuse it with a modern meaning. He first advocated it in order to give a highbrow and attractive aspect to his attack upon the dry laws, but he has had to refurbish it with each new merger or moratorium, with each new neglect of natural responsibilities by a slothful set of States.

His panacea is strikingly simple—almost too simple. It means anything—or nothing.

It is his only remedy for all the ills which beset the United States. Yet he must twist and squirm to escape its unfortunate implications. He finds it almost impossible to avoid the criticism that he favors political anarchy on the one hand, or a laissez-faire subservience to industrial dictatorship on the other. His proposed system of political feudalism is, indeed, difficult to defend.

In vagueness lies his one hope of victory, and he is victoriously vague.

Having no issue other than this sentimental shibboleth, he stirs only indirect interest in his ambition. But he deserves credit, perhaps, in that, as Governor of so small and uninfluential a State, he has been mentioned in the headlines at all. It is no reflection to suggest that there would be fewer headlines were he less handsome.

He is the Adonis of candidates. He once captured a handsomest-man contest conducted by a Baltimore newspaper. Were Presidents chosen for their good looks, there would be no need of an election.

He comes by his historical issue rightfully, however, even though he overemphasizes it. He gets it from his birth of Virginia-Maryland ancestry, his guarded bringing-up and his eminently correct career. He has never been exposed to more throbbing or tempestuous problems than the niceties involved in determining the proper relationship between the States and the Federal Government.

He is a political academe and Adamite.

ALBERT C. RITCHIE

He looks the part. He is a handsome but humorless figure, with a stiff and serious manner and mien toward all except the chummy coterie which dares to address him as "Bert." He has never been known, or even thought of, as "Al." Even toward his candidacy he assumes a detached and dignified attitude. Emotion or enthusiasm never rumple his fine, grey plume, cloud his clear, blue eyes or disturb his regular features.

Politically, he is the apostle of the primitive. He thinks that the clock of history can be turned back as if by a miracle—or by his election. He faces the problems of an increasingly complex civilization by directing his gaze toward the social and economic order of the last century—an age in which his philosophy might have had some significance.

He yearns audibly for that ancient, utopian era; he speaks eloquently of its "free men and free women."

He is, as Governor, simply an overseer; it is all he pretends to be. If he reaches the White House, he will retain that same, simple sense of official duty and responsibility. He will be a careful, competent, calculating keeper of the great seal and records.

Except that he is far more able and looks more

like a President ought to look, he would be a Democratic Calvin Coolidge.

He is, in short, a politician of the plantation period—the perfect product of his heredity and environment.

Only the State of Maryland could produce such a distinguished Diogenes.

Like its Chief Executive, Maryland is a compact and self-contained body. It has passed a shut-in and isolated existence, taking dramatic events of the nation's history—the Civil War, the Eighteenth Amendment, the threatening advance of industrial forces—with exceeding calm. Like Mr. Ritchie, it has striven painfully to achieve a pose and place that would be uniquely dispassionate alongside the hysterics of its sob-sister States.

Dubbed the "Free State" by merry, Menckenque leader-writers on the Baltimore *Evening Sun,* it has made a boast of that bit of buffoonery. It is, in all respects, a Graustarkian province, and Mr. Ritchie is its Prince.

It has waged a hilarious war against prohibition. But the outcome is only an alcoholic armistice. The Governor, appropriately, is the ideal commander for an army in armistice—for forces in suspended animation—even though he lacks the hilarity of

ALBERT C. RITCHIE

his troops. Both he and his State can point to an honorable history, but to one amazingly empty of emotion or drama.

At Annapolis, his colonial Capital, he acquires daily inspiration for his political text. The quaint, little town has changed but little since revolutionary days, in appearance or in contact with national forces. It has no trolleys, no city planning, no keen civic sense. Topsy had more direction in her growth.

It is peopled by what Mr. Ritchie calls "free men and free women." On the occasion of his inaugurations the townsfolk demonstrate what they mean by the Ritchie form of freedom. They overrun his beautiful, red-brick Executive Mansion with a revolutionary disrespect. I sometimes wonder what the stately and correct Governor, in gazing on this mad movie-mob scene, thinks of his theory of individual liberty, States' Rights—and "free men and women."

In Annapolis it apparently means license to strip the Governor's home of food and flowers reserved for gubernatorial guests. It means a jocose familiarity with "Our Bert" from which he seems to shrink. It bespeaks a quaint attitude toward government and Governors. I doubt if he appreciates the democratic and Jacksonian spirit shown by the citizenry in honor of his election at their careless hands.

It most assuredly does not symbolize that individual restraint which, as all his State papers say, must form the basis of his system of States' Rights and local self-government. Though he cannot abandon it without renouncing his ambition—for he has no other issue—his finely spun theory collapses under his troubled, blue eyes and upon his own threshold.

It is hard to believe that he does not discern the unworkability of his program for a sharper separation between the units which make up the American Union, for the transfer of more responsibility from the Central Government to States which will not shoulder existing burdens.

The Maryland Governor, for instance, is a frank foe of prohibition. He was thumbing his Grecian nose at Republican, presidential sponsors long before other Democrats, notably Franklin D. Roosevelt of New York, took this issue away from him. Nevertheless, he has approved fifteen county prohibition measures simply because the people of those areas desired legal aridity.

ALBERT C. RITCHIE

It was not, under his theory, his duty to reason why or wherefor—simply to sign.

His defense does him some discredit. His attitude represents a negation of intelligent government. It represents, as he sometimes senses, an evasion of problems which a changing order is producing for control and solution by a more decent and honest breed of men at Washington. It is, obviously, an absurd refinement of the democratic, or even representative, theory of government.

The people have not yet proved themselves to be the prophetic agencies of a discerning divinity that he believes them to be. In fact, his utterances on the subject of popular rule are both arduous and ambiguous. He does not seem quite sound—or sincere—when he speaks on this question so vital to his own philosophy.

"The instinct of the masses," he would have us believe, "may be sounder than the instinct of the politically self-anointed. In fact, there is usually an element of sound sense and true instinct in every mass movement (sic).... Because public sentiment so often seems non-existent, or quiescent, or sterile, or foolish, or difficult to understand, we both underrate and overrate it. It may be passive and apparently impotent to-day, and be all-powerful tomorrow. . . .

"If the path of progress through democracy and liberalism is slow, if it must be tested out by trial and error, at least the path thus offered is the only one that is safe. If gradual processes are inevitable for democratic ideals, at least those processes are onward and upward."

This passage reveals Mr. Ritchie at his best and worst. The maudlin and muddied thinking, the inane identification of "democracy" with "liberalism," may be forgiven him for the trustfulness which he shows toward his fellows. But he should not be disappointed if he finds few to share a trust which, in envisaging progress "onward and upward," tolerates so much passivity, foolishness, slowness, safeness, trial and error.

He believes, perhaps sincerely, that he stands upon sure and high ground, but his States' Rights doctrine does not meet the test of his own intellect. When he is asked to say where the division falls between Federal and State responsibility, he replies:

"It may seem difficult to draw the line, but you can tell pretty surely with each specific issue."

His own State of Maryland, for all his denuncia-

ALBERT C. RITCHIE

tion of the "fifty-fifty" system as subversive of State sovereignty, accepts federal financial assistance in several fields. It may pain him, and he may protest, but he accepts the devastating dole lest Maryland miss out.

Where he has invoked his philosophy to deny or rescind State aid to counties, it has caused crippling of essential activities. Several sections of Maryland are doing without proper hospital and transportation facilities in order that its presidential prospect may remain constant to his preachments of undiluted and undiminished home rule.

Mr. Ritchie, of course, submits no positive program; he simply voices a challenge. In fact, he makes a pathetic picture as he deprecates those developments which have transformed the thirteen colonies—among which he might have been a great Governor—into a world power.

There is a wistful, though well-meaning note, in his inaugural cries for "equal access to the door of opportunity," "a chance to the underfellow," "a just share of the national wealth to the farmer."

These, obviously, are not specific remedies; there is no hewing of the line here. But if these read like the declamations of a scholar at a grammar school oratorical period on Friday afternoon, even more naïve is his suggestion of the basic difficulty.

"The catch-word of the hour is 'economics,'" he protests. "We speak of economic laws as if they were a part of the order of nature, even though there is almost universal disagreement as to what they are.

"Perhaps we test life too much by the economic yardstick."

Perhaps we do—outside the trolleyless town of Annapolis.

Perhaps the economic world is too much with us —outside the "Free State of Maryland."

It is the custom for candidates to resort to platitudes. In pleading for "equal access to the door of opportunity," the Governor is only following in the footsteps of such worthies as Messrs. Harding, Coolidge and Hoover. But even they, inept as they have been, never made such a confession of fear and failure as Mr. Ritchie does in his attempted escape from "economic laws."

This shrinking from harsh realities is characteristic. He is an arch-hesitator. Indeed, he appears to dread direct contact with people and their problems. A desire for a lonely and isolated state has apparently animated him ever since he deserted the

ALBERT C. RITCHIE

law courts at the age of twenty-seven to place himself in the guiding hands of a trio of political bosses in Baltimore.

A man can be lonely—or indulge his loneliness—at the top, as Mr. Hoover demonstrates.

Once, referring to his position as Chief Executive of a small and orderly State, Mr. Ritchie said:

"It is a job that anyone can handle. It is not like being Governor of New York or Pennsylvania, in which the Governor of necessity must delegate many of his duties to agents. Everybody in Maryland who wants to see me can see me, and I can see everybody I want to see. That makes it nice."

He isolates himself at Annapolis, and mires himself in routine work. Although he reaches his office late in the morning, he stays through without lunch and returns to his desk after dinner each evening. Long after Annapolis has become dark and dingy, the lights from his executive chamber twinkle through the town. In a day he exhausts three secretaries, who have almost as little home life and as few diverting interests as he.

He is a glorified clerk. He reads and answers all letters; his door is ever open to the yokelry. He writes all his own speeches and State documents, laboriously copying and correcting and rewriting, as well as the many articles he writes for the magazines. Often he replies to communications from cranks with elaborate expositions of policy, including therein quotations from the law and citations of court decisions.

It may be, as his friends insist, good politics that impels him to such detailed attention to office work and extra-curricular duties, but it is more likely due to his strange and unexplainable desire to occupy himself with a lotus-like form of activity.

He has definite but commonplace assets. He has been a competent Chief Executive. He has reorganized the State Government, managed its institutions well, built good roads and reduced expenses. He has been honest, capable, conscientious and painstaking. Insofar as he has been faithful in minutiae, he may, conceivably, be entitled to an essay at larger affairs. Unfortunately for him, the American people do not select their Chief Magistrates in accord with this divine decree.

Fate has withheld from him the opportunity it gave to Calvin Coolidge in the Boston police strike. He has espoused no far-sighted legislation as did Woodrow Wilson when the latter was Governor of New Jersey. He has staged no dramatic feuds with the bosses after the manner of Theodore Roosevelt

ALBERT C. RITCHIE

at Albany. He cannot campaign, as did Mr. Hoover, in the role of a peripatetic and prodigal son.

He must stand or fall by a tidy bit of housekeeping in one of the tiniest States of the Union. It is his misfortune that he lacks those qualities which might have inspired him to make Maryland a political laboratory for daring experiments in government, and himself the exponent of an ordered liberalism. There is—alas!—no drama or daring in him.

Only once did he come near to dramatizing himself and his issue. It was on the occasion of his second inauguration in 1923. The spirit of the Annapolis horde all but caught him, and in his first, formal espousal of his States' Rights dostrine he almost thundered. But he just missed greatness. It was, instead, grandiose, and he himself a Cyrano de Bergerac, as his language alone shows. He said:

"A great, a fundamental, an enduring principle is at stake. No question of sectional advantage, of group gain, of party benefit or class. But a principle which reaches back through the ages, past the industrial and economic eras and the mighty wars which have made our country great, straight to the heart of civilization. . . . That principle calls for an end to centralization."

He did not, however, transport anybody beyond the events which have outdated his philosophy, "straight to the heart of civilization." Maryland cheers these perorations, chuckles over his annual nose-thumbings at Republican Presidents and elects him four times to an office never before refilled by the same man. It likes its Prince, no doubt of that.

He has had two other great opportunities—and missed miserably.

In 1924, when Alfred Emanuel Smith and William Gibbs McAdoo clashed at Madison Square Garden, he might conceivably have emerged as a compromise candidate. He was then a wet, it is true, but he had already begun to elevate himself from a highball to a highbrow level. He had more dignity and fewer enemies than Mr. Smith, less fanaticism than Mr. McAdoo.

So his advisers begged that he permit himself to be placed in nomination with a compelling challenge, and his name kept before the convention for the duration of the struggle. Had he acquiesced, and had the strategy been successful, the brawls of ballots that insured a Republican triumph even

ALBERT C. RITCHIE

in the wake of the oil scandals might have been avoided.

But the careful, cautious, conservative Mr. Ritchie decreed otherwise. Whether he was moved by instinctive conservatism or characteristic distaste for a fight matters not. He was presented to the party as a middle-of-the-road man, and it was impossible to determine which road he meant to travel.

He might have been the darling of the Board of Temperance, Prohibition and Public Morals of the Methodist Episcopal Church, insofar as the nominating tender revealed him or expressed his philosophy. He might have been seeking second place on Mr. Coolidge's Republican ticket.

The result was that he did not become even a dark horse. He was, rather, a white horse upon which even the Lady Godiva might have ridden without a sense of shame.

So it has been and always will be. The event is typical of his career, character and candidacy.

Always he lags and loafs and lets down his admirers.

Likewise he declined to inaugurate an experiment which might have entitled him to greater consideration than he may receive. Despite a widespread

THE MIRRORS OF 1932

demand that Maryland develop the vast waterpower resources at Conowingo, he preferred to turn it over to private interests.

The project, he said in dismissing popular petitions, would cost more than the State could afford. Moreover, he is stubbornly opposed to public participation in any business that competes with private industry. He raised objections which might have fallen from the lips of Mr. Hoover.

Had he been moved—or able—to adopt a contrary course in the power and prohibition controversies, it is quite possible that his vitalization of these two dominant issues of 1932 might have enhanced his availability. Certain it is that he would not have been left with nothing more stable or sensational to recommend him than a prize-winning countenance and a platform clipped from frayed and dog-eared text books.

The Governor is too cautious and conservative, if not too reactionary, for his own good. He is a follower rather than a leader, a pedant rather than a pioneer. Despite his four terms in a high and honorable office, his only product has been so much paper work, so many new miles of roads, slightly smaller budgets.

He will, clearly, bring no daring or dynamic ideas

ALBERT C. RITCHIE

to the presidency, should he achieve it. He will be simply another well-intentioned conservative. He does not feel deeply or concern himself with the burdens which may afflict the masses. He does not conceive it to be the government's duty to provide any relief other than "equal access to the door of opportunity."

He will be safe and sound, but neither brilliant nor forward-looking. He will sponsor reaction rather than reform. He possesses, too, the Hamlet-like strain which the country has found so exasperating in Mr. Hoover. He is slow to reach decisions, and he vacillates between policies. He is even tardy in getting to his office.

Although opinions differ on this point, he impresses many as cold and calculating, selfish and unappreciative. His sharpest critics hold him to be insincere, and there is some evidence in his lack of fire that nothing touches him deeply. Albeit reiteration may have begat conviction, his maneuvers to keep his States' Rights issue abreast of the times indicate shallowness as well as some dissembling.

The principal change resulting from a transfer of the presidency from Mr. Hoover to him would be that the Democrats would distribute the patronage.

THE MIRRORS OF 1932

He looks good but he does not measure up to his looks. He does not quite ring true.

Yet there is an engaging quality in the frankness with which he admits his desire to be President. He would love the honor and glory, and he says so with a bluntness unusual in present-day politics. He accepts all invitations to further his candidacy, whether it means speech-making in distant places or presentation of his views in the magazines and newspapers.

He dismisses tourist-visitors to the Executive Mansion with the disarming wish that he may soon receive them "in the East Room of the White House." With persistence, but also with dignity, he seeks to attach important persons to his train, and he contents himself with the thought that he may be the second choice of such tycoons as National Chairman Johnnie Raskob and "Barney" Baruch.

It is like him to rely upon secondary strength for the realization of the dearest desire a man may cherish.

He is much the same man in private life that the public glimpses.

Although his birth, breeding and political eminence entitle him to lead colonial cotillions, he

ALBERT C. RITCHIE

shuns formal society. When he is not cloistered at Annapolis, he joins a few old cronies at a Baltimore Club for a comfortable "chin." He enjoys most a sail down Chesapeake Bay in the flagship of Maryland's oyster armada, with a few good fellows sitting about and a good breeze blowing for his "free men."

He cannot, if he would, be a hail-fellow-well-met. He is, mentally and physically, a recluse, though not an ostentatious one. He takes no exercise other than infrequent indulgence in solitary squash; he depends upon baths at a Baltimore physical culture school to keep his slender, tapering, dancing master's body in good shape. He talks and reads only of subjects pertaining to politics and government; he is a governmental grind.

Oddly enough, his choice among recent books is Siegfried's "America Comes of Age." More in tune with his political sentimentalism is his favorite among ballads—"When You and I Were Young, Maggie."

It would be quite unfair to underestimate the Marylander's abilities or attainments, however. It would be impolitic to minimize his undoubted attraction to an element of the electorate which may dominate the next election as it did the 1928 struggle—the women. With them this stately and handsome fellow has undeniable strength, all the more so because he happens to be unmarried.

No less an authority than Mary Garden bears witness to his quiet charm. The famous diva, who never visits Baltimore without having him to lunch, says of her hero:

"He is the cutest boy in America."

OWEN D. YOUNG

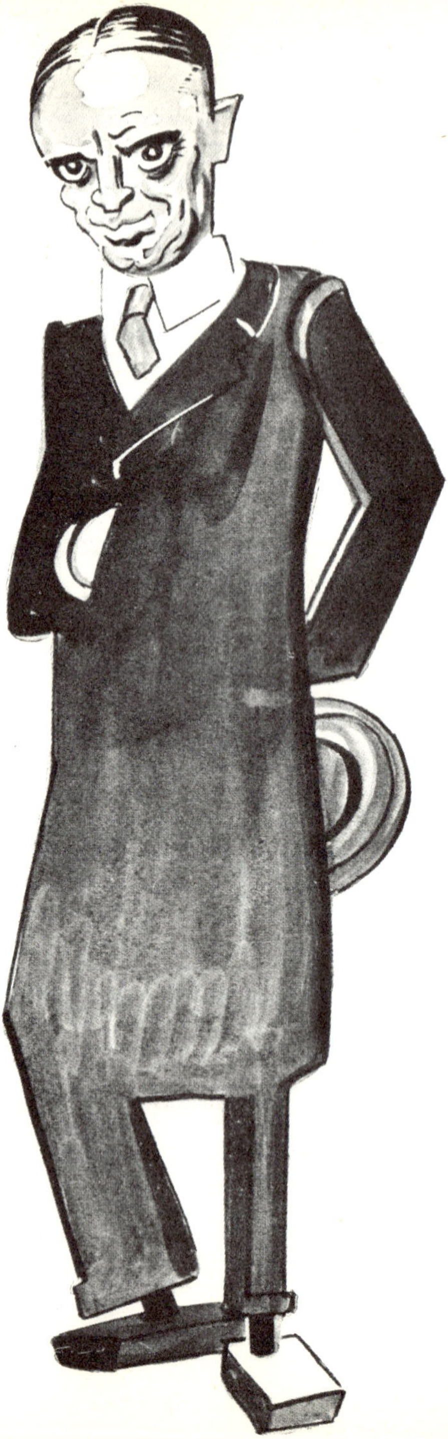

OWEN D. YOUNG

Owen D. Young is our first world citizen.

If it is not in the nature of a slight to consider him for so petty an office as the presidency, it is assuredly shameful to suggest that he associate with such a lesser breed of men as politicians—for whom he expresses the utmost disdain each time he stoops to slam them.

No party's philosophy is sufficiently circumferential to encompass him, no party's platform sufficiently Olympian to reach the rarefied atmosphere in which he glides toward a unique Utopia.

By comparison with this Cortez of Capital, Woodrow Wilson was a simple villager and a rabid nationalist. The late apostle of universal loving-kindness, not even in his most intoxicating moments, suffered so much from international inebriety.

Mr. Wilson died while pleading for American adherence to the League of Nations, and the Democratic Party almost died with him. It is, therefore, ironical that the funereal faction of Wilsonists should be Mr. Young's presidential sponsors.

It is an even more powerful League which their new hero has created. The mighty forces which he controls—massed wealth, radio, power and assorted industries—threaten to sweep politics and politicians from the stage. Indeed, that is his ideal. In all his addresses he urges that politics and nationalism be supplanted by economics and internationalism.

The country boy who never rode on a street car until he was full-grown enjoys an influence possessed by few men of past and present. He outranks most military, political and economic figures of history.

It is no mere coincidence that one of his most precious possessions is a globe of the world, and that the study of globular geography fascinates him. He keeps a globe at his downtown office in New York City, at his town house on Park Avenue and at his country estate in Connecticut. It is his daily inspiration.

As he twirls the sphere on its axis, nations dwindle to scant specks and merge. All sectional and sentimental boundaries vanish. Mankind be-

OWEN D. YOUNG

comes a revolving mass—man a robot—and society a mere mechanized existence.

Under the bland and beneficent workings of this ultimate Young Plan neither nation nor individual would have the right—or the happiness—of getting out of gear. Everywhere there would be "control and centralization"—his formulae for all problems.

Far more effectively than Herbert Hoover, who pays him the compliment of plagiarizing regularly upon his preachments, Mr. Young represents new and ruthless forces. He symbolizes the mechanical and materialistic spirit of the age, and the man in the White House is not even his minor prophet.

Like his two handmaidens—Radio and Power—he heads toward an era in which slavery shall become more economic than political—in which the chain gang of humanity shall move in a maze of chain stores, chain banks, chain hydroelectric systems, chain broadcasting programs—in which the spirit of nationalism and individualism shall no longer constitute a challenge to "King Owen the First."

The Democrats, of course, cannot afford to nominate such a man for the presidency. Nor would they entertain the idea were it not that Mr. Young is a most artful and attractive propagandist.

THE MIRRORS OF 1932

Unlike his archtype, John D. Rockefeller, he needs no Ivy Lee to appease a resentful populace. He has elevated publicity, corporate and personal, to the plane of a philosophy. Whereas Mr. Rockefeller distributes shiny dimes to expiate his past, Mr. Young sheds shiny statements to win benediction for his present purposes.

He is no gawky and growling person such as Mr. Rockefeller was in the days when the latter was building the oil trust. Mr. Young is charming and disarming, cultured and soft-spoken. He appeals with religious fervor for the payment of a "cultural wage," thus putting the "full dinner pail" on the shelf. He warns his associates that they must be fair to Labor even while his own corporation—the General Electric Company—maintains an open shop. He expounds such admirable theories that Wall Street, now and then, has shuddered at his radical tendencies.

Yet Mr. Rockefeller, basically, has as much claim to White House honors as Mr. Young. They are two of a kind in the presidential pod.

The only difference is that Mr. Young is far more successful in persuading the public of his high and holy ideals. He has talked himself to the pedestal of an industrial demigod, and an awed silence permits him to preserve his pose.

OWEN D. YOUNG

He is, in the popular mind, one of our Better Business Men. He occupies pulpits and delivers baccalaureate sermons. At the Capital there is a church plaque and tower named for him in tribute to his services to humanity. The Universalists, appropriately enough, have canonized him.

He lives the good, the simple, the kindly life. All the homely virtues are his. He is an intellectual, and for this much may be forgiven in a day which has given us Herbert Hoover and "Jimmie" Walker in high place.

He collects first editions of Victorian novelists, he abides in bookshops and art galleries, he studies the European scene from a hidden garret in Paris. He visits cathedrals by moonlight as a rest from Dawes Plan sessions and conferences called to create an international radio monopoly. He lays brick for country schoolhouses with his own hands, and praises the austere life.

He smokes a pipe, rides the subway, nibbles a sandwich for lunch, avoids all unseemly display. He is unhurried and uncombustible—rare traits in the modern industrialist. He can be, if it pleases him, gallant, wistful, even naïve, and personable.

He is a balanced and brainy individual. In ability and personality he stands far above most of the candidates for the presidential nomination in both major parties. He is the sort of man of whom Lloyd George said, more than ten years ago:

"Before I die, I expect to see him President of the United States."

He exhibits few of the qualities of the Babbitt, although he may be characterized as our first super-Babbitt. If his talk seems to have naught in common with those of Rotary songsters, it is solely because it is of things still mysterious to an age in transition.

It may not be long, however, ere the stuff of which his universe is made—dynamos, radio, cross-licensing agreements, patent pools—occupies a place in our ideology akin to the things which Sinclair Lewis made both imbecilic and immortal.

If Mr. Young is as yet only a dim and delightful figure to the public, it is because the man cannot be seen for the machine.

There are even more definite—and significant—reasons. He detests ordinary publicity; he cannot endure its sharp and pitiless lines. Biographers cannot approach him, in the flesh or in the spirit. His associates safeguard him from too deep or disillusioning a scrutiny. Though they furnish libraries of data anent his industrial accomplishments, they draw a charmed circle about him.

OWEN D. YOUNG

Thus his personality has captured the popular imagination, until now he is proclaimed as the Miracle Man of an Enlightened Big Business. Thus his pious pronouncements disarm an uncritical public and obstruct a clear view of the man.

He has been accepted at his own verbal evaluation so long that he is deemed to be not only the expounder but also the author of the Golden Rule. The beautiful Spirit of Service animates him, in his daily doxology. Rosaries of sweet and succulent words fall trippingly from his tongue—sweet and sweeping statements with which nobody can disagree.

He is the Santa Claus of modern Industry and Business.

It is almost incredible that Mr. Young has been taken at his word—or words. It is almost unbelievable that in this age of scepticism his unctuous utterances have not been measured—or contrasted—with his performances.

It may be due to the fact that Mr. Young is not consciously insincere. He doubtless has faith in his own high purposes. There is reason to suspect, however, that he does not permit his itinerant ideals to influence his economic and industrial policies and programs.

His sermons, for all their smoothness and sweetness, fall upon stony ears within his corporate circle. Only the public—and some politicians—are fooled.

The fair conclusion is that Mr. Young is an idealistic but ineffectual individual—which nobody credits—or that he is no more than an ornate and oracular façade.

Certain it is that behind this fine front there have been perpetrated practices which do not square with his preachments. The power trust, for example, has been severely condemned by the very people who profess admiration for Mr. Young. It would be unfair to assess all its sins against him, but there is no doubt that, did he exert himself, he could make his words to shine among the men and corporations which compose it.

The magnates who sit upon its board of strategy are his friends, his admirers, his associates. As one of our first public utilitarians, he is their unofficial Nestor. He addresses their conventions, volunteering sage and sound advice, as always. He is the outstanding figure of the electrical industry —its prophet and publicist.

Passing over the power trust's economic evils— which are many—it was this organization which incurred the condemnation of public opinion in recent years. It was this group which financed newspapers secretly, instituted indecent lobbies, rewrote collegiate textbooks, subsidized impoverished college professors, crept into the churches, engaged former statesmen as proselyters, and, for a while, threatened to propagandize every stream of human thought for their own interests.

When these facts were developed on the Senate floor and before the Federal Trade Commission, the power trust had no defenders in the houses of its friends. Even within the walls of Congress and Legislatures usually susceptible to vested influence there was none to excuse or explain.

For once, our apostle of the decencies was still. He voiced no protest. He was as silent a propagandist then as he had been a false prophet on the eve of the government's investigation.

Had the sponsors of the inquiry—Senators Thomas J. Walsh of Montana and George W. Norris of Nebraska—been content with Mr. Young's say-so, there would never have been an official exposure of the power trust. For Mr. Young, in an address before the National Electric Light Association—which conducted the campaign to control all channels of public opinion—announced that a new era of good feeling between utilities and the public had arrived.

In his most public-spirited vein he declared that consumers and corporations no longer conceived their interests to be antagonistic. In consequence, he asserted, the sinister efforts of public utilities to pack Legislatures and dominate legislation had "almost disappeared."

Inasmuch as governmental disclosures of the persistence of these practices echoed and reechoed to the Young platitudes through the next four years—from 1926 to 1930—his fine words hardly depicted reality. There is thus suggested the awful suspicion that he did not know what was going on about him, or that he did not care.

Where, it is pertinent to ask, was the preacher, the philosopher and the philanthropist in the days when the program of propaganda which he deprecated was formulated and executed!

It is a fair interrogation. It is one which the Democrats must be prepared to meet if they present Mr. Young for the presidency.

His radio trust is even now under attack by several arms of the government. The Department of Justice has asked its dissolution on the ground that it is an "unlawful combination, conspiracy and monopoly." It has already been adjudged, in effect, to be guilty of a violation of the anti-trust laws. Volumes of testimony before senatorial committees and courts and government commissions picture it as having sought ruthlessly to dominate the national and international radio fields.

Without regard for the merits of this maze of legal controversies, it is unfortunate for Mr. Young's political ambitions that they will be in progress during the period when the Democrats select their candidate. More important still, the attack lies against his underlying legal and economic philosophy.

The corporations which make up his $7,000,000,000 radio combine are only incidental in any study of the man; they are simply manifestations of the higher ethics and intelligence of Owen D. Young.

In short, the world citizen is on trial. The long legal battle in prospect will determine whether his economic structure can long endure.

He, of course, believes that it can and should. On the senatorial witness stand he has frequently expressed the conviction that the system of communications should be a monopoly—"public or private." His attitude was reflected even more boldly in the response which the Radio Corporation of America filed with the Federal Trade Commission some years ago.

The argument consisted of an excerpt from an address delivered by Chief Justice Charles Evans Hughes in 1918. Had this appeal been produced in time, it might have prevented the return of Mr. Hughes to the Supreme Court. Now it may simply affect Mr. Young's preferment, especially as the Hughes doctrine was described as "the present position of the respondents."

"Is it too much," asked Mr. Hughes, "to expect that we shall have a saner attitude toward business, toward the necessary activities which afford the basis of progress? I hope that the days devoted to the application of the uncertainties of the Sherman Act are numbered."

There speaks the unguarded voice of Owen D. Young. With all respect to "Johnnie" Raskob, I doubt if it can ever be the ground upon which the Democratic Party will choose to wage its presidential battles.

In view of all this, it is interesting to recall what Mr. Young said as class orator upon graduation from Boston University Law School in 1896.

"Never before in the history of English law,"

he declared, "has the incitement to swerve from principle been so great.

"The régime of anarchy on the one hand and of centralized power and corporate wealth on the other, are dangerous to a stable equilibrium and a constant rule.

"Our Legislatures are making much law that is little more than a series of concessions, confessions and compromises. . . .

"The great lawyer of the future will be the man who has the faculty for seeing right; the man who has the courage to tell what he saw; the man who has the stability to maintain what he said."

Mr. Young's career since he uttered that adolescent challenge does not present the study of a man suddenly succumbing to the allure of high finance. His has been a persistent progress toward natural culmination in the formation of the world's greatest monopoly.

He was one of the pioneers in the application of law to Big Business. As counsel for numerous banks and trust companies in Boston, his firm faced the problem of salvaging assets of small and bankrupt power companies. It was he who rescued and reorganized them into strong and centralized corporations. He furnished the legal advice and super-

THE MIRRORS OF 1932

vision for some of the first mergers, reorganizations and expansions which are now so common an occurrence with him.

He mastered the higher mathematics—and morality—of corporate financing and organization. Neither sensational nor scintillating, he hardly ever entered the courtroom. It was true of him then, as it is now, that he excelled in conference. His suave and imperturbable manner won friend and disarmed foe, as it still does.

He thought more than he spoke. He has a great ability for grasping the essentials of an opponent's case even more clearly than they do. He has the rare faculty of discovering in advance what is in the other fellow's mind, and what arguments he must use. His own thoughts he conceals behind an altarlike brow, too luminous eyes, a poker smile and an unequalled urbanity.

In many of these prophetic struggles for supremacy in the young power industry he bested better known attorneys for the General Electric Company, and in 1913 he was offered the post of vice-president and general counsel in that concern. In retrospect, he says that it pained him to leave Boston, where he had been wont to frequent the bookshops and lecture in the law school. But—

characteristically—he wanted money, and he went where money was.

The General Electric Company as now constituted is his creation. It was a sprawling and disorganized corporation when he joined it—powerful in the manufacturing end but weak in the distributing field. He stood in the midst of the scene, and straightway reorganized and strengthened every part of the structure.

Without delay he inaugurated a movement to capture personal and corporate good will. It is typical of him that he envisaged his industry as an empire which, like any political entity or super-government, must have an ambassador for the maintenance of diplomatic relations with the subject public. He has been the ambassador.

It has become almost a mania with him, as his extravagantly worded house orations to General Electric employees demonstrate.

"Every one," he once told them, "has bad mornings, hates to hear the phone ring or to see the office door open. I beg of you, gentlemen, when next you meet such a morning, take a stick of dynamite and blow up one of our plants. But do not take it out on a customer of the General Electric.

"We can replace the plant you have destroyed. We know its value, and we have a reserve from which we can rebuild. But we cannot measure the good will you have destroyed, and we cannot know if we have replaced it."

There, mayhap, is the whole secret of his fine and fair words. It is good business.

He is, most obviously, a remarkable individual. But should the Democrats succumb to his personality and his preachings, they will learn, too late, that he is their most vulnerable candidate. They will discover that they need more than polished phrases in the man they present as a possible President. They will play into the trembling hands of Mr. Young's less able and less articulate counterpart—Herbert Hoover.

The nomination of Mr. Young would be a desertion and a repudiation of the Democrats' historic traditions.

Even Mr. Hoover, who dare not move in any direction, might be preferable to those who think there is a spirit worth preservation in our existing social and economic system. For Mr. Young would move. He would swing, slyly but swiftly, into a mad dance of monopoly at home and internationalism abroad.

OWEN D. YOUNG

He would combine the worst features of William McKinley and Woodrow Wilson. His election would hasten the day when a strong and victorious third party might arise in the land.

He would be a benevolent despot, it is true, but still a despot. The blood of dictators runs in his veins. His favorite expression is "centralized control," rivalling Mr. Hoover's fondness for "efficiency."

Seemingly unimportant events reveal his dictatorial makeup. Although he electrified his birthplace of Van Hornesville, N. Y., at his own expense, he located the control switch in his parental home, and when bedtime came for that dwelling place, darkness also descended upon all the villagers.

At his Alma Mater, St. Lawrence University, toward which he stands as trustee and benefactor, he dominates the collegiate scheme. He has even prescribed a course of extracurricular reading, and, he insists, those who neglect his literary dictates cannot be called cultured.

It is not surprising, therefore, that he detests and distrusts politicians. Again and again he pleads for a "holiday of parliaments" in order that economic forces may be permitted free play. His disdain for the system under which we are governed—or misgoverned—is supreme.

"I shall be happy," he says, "if we can substitute the calm findings of the investigator for the blatant explosions of the politicians. I beg the politicians and statesmen to stop their harmful talk until the facts are found."

Or, more superciliously—

"Our politics and our economics are in conflict everywhere in the world to-day. . . . The forces are violent and imposing. Some better way must be found, accommodating each to the other or they will destroy themselves.

"In some European countries the question is being seriously discussed of providing economic parliaments in addition to the political ones in order that men especially qualified for the handling of those problems may deal with them. . . .

"It has even been suggested that, if a holiday on armaments is good, a holiday of parliaments will be better."

The politicians would sign their death warrant if they gave him even a modicum of political authority. The considerations—both the petty and the profound—which move them do not interest him. The understanding of human values that must enter into the writing and enforcement of all law is missing in him.

What Mr. Young does not, and cannot sense, is that the makers of our statutes and the moulders of our institutions must be swayed by thought of human nature's frailties, prejudices and sensibilities as well as by recognition of vice and virtue writ in larger letters.

Legislators and executives in a democracy should not be, as is Mr. Young, "too bright or good for human nature's daily food."

They cannot, for instance, write the sort of bonus law measure which he suggested at the Capital. Proceeding along cold and businesslike lines—the sort which he would adopt in the White House—he proposed a bill under which every ex-soldier would have been required to sign what amounted to a pauper's oath.

Even his International Bank, which was designed to fill an economic want, has become the plaything of continental politics. His famed reparations plan is crumbling.

Mr. Young has a great deal to learn.

In a democracy there is no royal road—or short circuit—to the Utopia which he envisages.

Nobody recognizes his political incapacity more

than himself. He concedes his total lack of qualifications for the presidency. Of the proposal to place him in the White House he says:

"To administer political affairs successfully requires political knowledge and political experience. I have neither. I have never taken a job for which my experience did not in some degree qualify me, and I hope I never may."

This, I imagine, is one of those intuitive reactions which Mr. Young describes as "a hunch in the seat of my pants."

NEWTON DIEHL BAKER

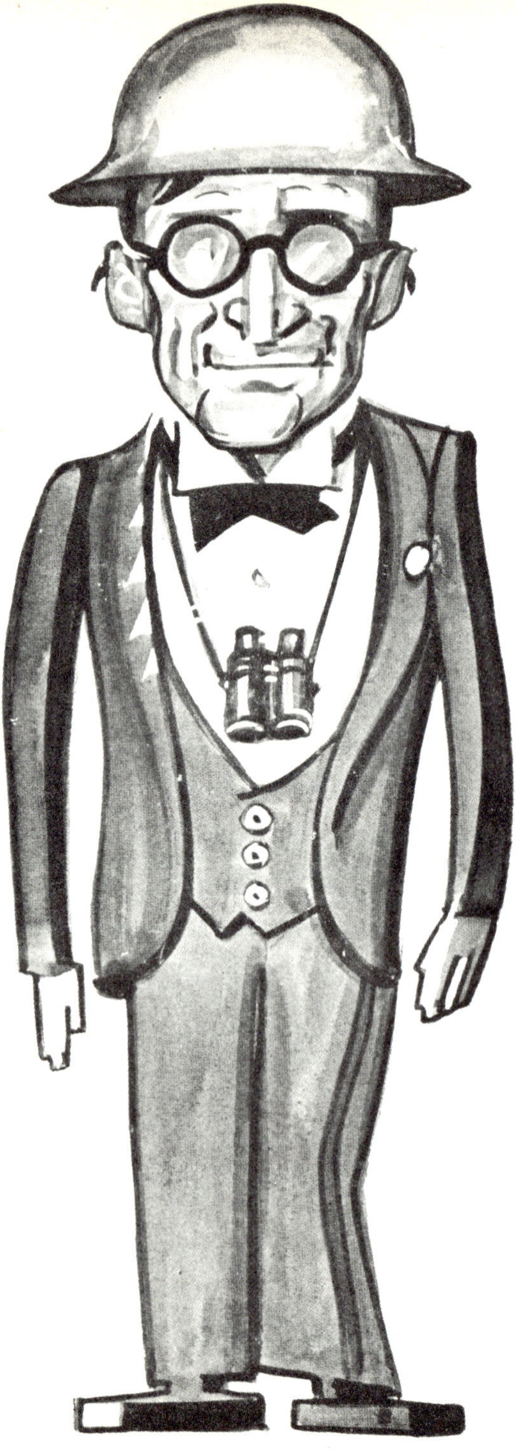

NEWTON D. BAKER

ALL that Newton D. Baker needs to make him of presidential stature is a few more inches in height.

It is ironic that one of the best minds of the generation—culturally, legally, socially, economically—should be housed in so unimpressive a body. He has the head of a George Bernard Shaw—his favorite modern writer—and the physique of an undersized undergraduate; it gives him the appearance of topheaviness. He still seems more of an "angel child"—the nickname of his boyhood—than a statesman.

"Pansy Baker" the Washington correspondents dubbed him on the day he took office as Secretary of War. Despite gradual recognition of his great ability and his even greater potentialities, "Pansy Baker" he remains to Capital circles.

"Pansied idealism" was his foes' sneering characterization of his administration as reform Mayor of Cleveland in his younger days, and Theodore Roosevelt translated this description into that of "exquisitely unfit" during the stormy days of 1918. He has been unable to escape these sobriquets, largely because he lacks those few extra inches.

Many years ago, when he went along with a group of college students to seek assignment as supers in a Shakesperean production, the stage manager shoved him roughly aside.

"There are no Cupids in this show," remarked the showman.

Politics is like the theater. A false and tinselled scale of values prevails.

The American people, I imagine, still regard Mr. Baker as a "Cupid"—who sought to win the World War with darts—as a pacifist who headed the greatest war machine in history—as a most excellent person but hardly the sort to choose as Chief Executive.

This is an entirely erroneous impression. He is, by far, the ablest candidate for the presidency in the two major parties. The most brilliant member of the official family Woodrow Wilson assembled, he is, in many respects, better equipped for the White House than the Princeton professor was in 1912.

NEWTON D. BAKER

He might be the product of the schooling which Plato prescribes for the rulers of the Republic. He is steeped in the classics, economics, history; he enjoys a historical perspective rare in our Presidents; he has a social conscience so keen that it led him to enrol in the ranks of that prince of politicians, the late Tom Johnson of Cleveland; he translated his social creed into reality as Mayor of Cleveland; though a professing pacifist, he ranks among our greatest Secretaries of War.

He is humble and honest.

"I will do my best," he smiled wistfully when he was named Secretary of War, "but I have much to learn; for, even as a child, I did not play with lead soldiers."

He is practical, even hard-boiled, yet he says of himself:

"I am a dreamer of dreams."

His very strength is his weakness. A man of prodigious intellect and learning, it is impossible for him to realize that the aged food upon which he has been raised is too strong for the stomachs of hustling America. His readiness to discuss present-day problems in their proper perspective subjects him to severe attacks. Although he does not look down condescendingly upon the American scene, he cannot conceal his impersonal and historical viewpoint.

He has, for instance, dedicated himself to advance of his dead leader's cause—the League of Nations. He rarely delivers a speech, no matter how trivial the subject, without eulogizing the international ideal. At the Madison Square Garden convention he stirred the delegates to frenzy with his appeal for a pro-League plank.

It was as if Mr. Baker, gazing down into the grave, were keeping a pledge and a troth with Woodrow Wilson. Even the newspaper correspondents brushed the tears from their eyes and leaped to their feet.

If he were told that he might have the Democratic presidential nomination, provided he abandoned this crusade, he would refuse the offer. There is little of selfish ambition in him—so little that it is difficult to understand the man.

He assumes this same objective attitude toward himself. Perhaps no man is so self-critical, so intensely introspective.

He "could not face a casualty list," they said, yet he forced himself to. Whereas Woodrow Wilson, Theodore Roosevelt, Calvin Coolidge even, with honest heroics, would have mounted the

NEWTON D. BAKER

White House roof in such moments, if only to clench their fists and shout their emotions to the skies, the boyish figure in the War Department simply sat back limply, grasped the sides of his chair so hard the blood showed in his fingers and bit his thin lips.

He can be as emotional as he is intellectual—but his emotions, with the exception of that time in Madison Square Garden, are ever under control.

Many a time, before dawn, when called to his telephone by members of the General Staff, excited correspondents, by Wilson, to listen to fateful news from overseas, he displayed a coolness which became the wonder of the Capital.

"Yes," his quiet voice would answer, "this is Baker. How do you do?"

While the Daughters of the American Revolution, Messrs. Roosevelt and Hughes and half the Congress assailed him as a pacifist, he subjected himself to an even more severe cross-examination. Mid-winter of 1918 found him in the front-line trenches, at advanced hospital stations, upon bleak ground swept by men and munitions he had despatched across the seas.

"Newton D. Baker," he soliloquized, "what are you doing here? You—a pacifist—taking part in a war—this war—sending men to their death—and calling for more men—and munitions."

And to himself he answered—a justification to which he may have felt those other critics had no right:

"Wherever there is a movement to end war—to hasten the day when war will be no more—Newton D. Baker will be in it."

At the Capital he was a curious figure—for a Secretary of War. Whenever he had a moment to himself, free from the General Staff, the War Industries Board, foreign military missions, the Cabinet, he became a small figure huddled in some corner with his nose poked into a book. It might be a nonsense book, a Greek tragedy in the original, an early Latin comedy, a new treatise on economics, a novel by George Eliot, a lyric by Robert Browning—his favorite poet.

He was then—and is now—eminently sane. He dwelt in a realm of his own even during the blackest months of the war.

I doubt if the American electorate would appreciate him, even though it might elect him. There have been few men like Newton D. Baker in American history—few men who have been intellectual prodigy and practical politician, a

NEWTON D. BAKER

strange mingling of Athenian peripatetic and Ohio lawyer.

There are recesses of his mind which he rarely opens—perhaps because there are few to explore them with him. Therefore he creates the impression that he is not always quite frank. Perhaps he is not in the ordinary sense. It may be shyness, or it may be that too much learning has insulated him against friendship with ordinary folk.

What to think of a man who tried so awkwardly —and failed so miserably—to be natural that first day he met newspapermen en bloc in Cleveland. His friends had urged him to be hard-boiled, to put up a stiff, if not stuffed, front, and so his greeting was:

"God damn it, it's a nice day!"

Even cynical City Hall reporters were shocked to hear these familiar words fall from the lips of the official with the choir-boy manner and cherubic countenance.

Many years later, on the day he walked into the War Department building in 1916, he had a similar encounter with correspondents. There was, obviously, no news, and to make talk a correspondent referred to the bowl of pansies which friends had sent for the occasion of his swearing-in.

THE MIRRORS OF 1932

Then it was that Mr. Baker, like a character in a Hardy novel, fashioned his future insofar as the public estimate of it was concerned.

Sitting on one leg, while the other swung and missed the floor by inches, the new Secretary of War spoke eloquently of his passion for pansies. He fondled the flowers as he talked. He is, in a small way, a horticulturist, and pansies were, therefore, a legitimate topic.

As always, he spoke *Atlantic Monthly* English, and in an earnest and compelling manner. The contrast between the subject and style, combined with the circumstances under which he expanded on pansies, could not but stir the satire of his hearers.

"Pansy Baker!", they exclaimed as they left his office.

It is a measure of the man that, despite this inauspicious start and the fierce partisanship which swirled about him during the war, his worth has been recognized. As the years 1916–1919 recede, his ability as an administrator assumes large proportions.

Experienced military men who served under him have always been his admirers; it was only the populace which howled at him. Republican investigations have left him unscathed. America's military annals are emblazoned with no brighter pages than those which he helped to inscribe.

This, however, is undoubtedly a more impartial verdict than Republican publicists, reviving such ancient issues as pacifism, Teutonism and internationalism, would render if Mr. Baker becomes the Democrats' nominee. There are, to be sure, many ghosts to be drafted for service against him by the G.O.P.—memories of his radical municipal theories in Cleveland as well as of the prejudices directed against him in war days.

He has often been called upon to face such handicaps, however. He does not seem to mind them. He is too earnest, too immersed in the immediate job, to let them bother him.

There is an awful air of detachment about him. From a volume of Browning's sonnets he can leap into a political convention to still and subdue lowbrow politicians, as he once did in Ohio, and then return to his carefully marked page. He can suppress his shyness and sensitiveness, and even deeper feelings, if the effort seems worth while.

He is a sentimental Stoic.

His small size hurt him, but did not hinder him for long, in his first appearance upon the political stage. When he was sent to substitute for a popular spell-binder at a Cleveland ward meeting, he was mistaken for a messenger boy. When he explained that he was to deliver an address, the chairman looked down at him in amusement. The audience guffawed at the sight of this solemn, dark-haired, brown-eyed youngster.

"Well, come on, boy," commanded the chairman. "Tell us something."

What he told them, and how he told it, made him an immediate power in municipal politics.

It is characteristic of him that he became an admirer of Mayor Johnson, the political pugilist who was denounced as a demagogue and eulogized as a democrat in the early years of the century. Although public office held only small financial reward, Mr. Baker preferred it to lucrative offers from private corporations which competed for his services.

He devoted many years to this pioneer movement in liberal government of a municipality. With Johnson he fought for three-cent trolley fares, three-cent lighting charges, three-cent dance halls, publicly owned utility plants, a new home rule charter, public parks, municipal symphony orchestras.

It was Mr. Baker who enabled Johnson to effect many of these reforms. For years he almost lived

NEWTON D. BAKER

in the courtrooms of the city, State and nation—the Supreme Court of the United States. He fought fifty-five injunctions brought by the public utilities, and he won most of them. He also bested opponents of Cleveland's civic program in the Ohio Legislature.

He coined a new word—civitism—as an expression of the municipal spirit he sought to arouse, and he headed a movement for the coinage of a three-cent piece. He became known as "the three-cent Mayor." Cleveland, in those years, was his idol and his only interest. He rejected repeated offers to enter private practice, and he turned down Wilson's request that he become Secretary of the Interior in 1913.

"He was the youngest but the wisest member of my family," said Johnson.

He took time out, however, to champion Wilson's cause at the Baltimore convention in 1912. No more than a local figure then, his oratory led the convention to violate the traditional unit rule so that his twenty-one delegates from Cleveland could be cast for Wilson against Governor Judson Harmon of Ohio. During this same period he served with Justice Louis D. Brandeis as counsel for the National Consumers' League, and defended the constitutionality of many laws enacted in the public interest.

He was, through this period, the same shy, strange, intellectual Baker the nation came to know later. He forced the director of municipal music to change his programs from jazz to Wagner, Verdi, Donizetti.

As candidate for Mayor in 1911, he announced his political philosophy in the following words: "Lex citius tolerare vult privatum damnum quam publicum malum." When the street-car company made a seemingly attractive proposal, he replied: "Timeo Danaos et dona ferentes." It is little wonder that Cleveland considered him to be "the most intellectual Mayor in captivity."

Nevertheless, it reelected him in the year that saw Johnson's defeat. In 1911 it gave him the largest majority any candidate for the Mayoralty had ever received. He was as popular on the waterfront as he was on Euclid Avenue—the "Millionaires' Row" through which he built a trolley line in the face of protests from the privileged.

His public utility program, although highly advanced at that period, was not that of a political swashbuckler. He believes that the service of transportation, lighting, etc. constitute public conveniences which should not be conducted for profit. They furnish the basis for a well-ordered and comfortable society, in his opinion, and they should not be abused, although most susceptible to abuse. Yet he did not forget that unoffending stockholders were involved, and a return of 6 per cent. upon a generous estimate of investment was allowed.

Although he has become the attorney for large steel, industrial and railroad corporations since his retirement to private life, his views, as a public official, have changed little. He has in recent years defended the establishment of monopoly upon the basis of patent rights, but, within practical limits, his old philosophy would undoubtedly influence his policies if he should become President. It may be this phase of his career which causes alarm to interests which, in other respects, would be content to see him in the White House.

No cynic, despite some justification, he feels deep concern over recent trends in the social and political life of the United States.

The American people, in his opinion, have few deep roots or permanent relationships. Their contacts with the past and the present are brief and casual. As a solid basis of progress and persistence, there is insufficient education for service, insufficient devotion to traditions, insufficient ancestral restraints. The people are inarticulate, unmindful, there is no common impulse, and therefore no real force for improvement of conditions.

His thoughts are of interest not only for the light they throw upon him, but also because of his platonic viewpoint and his personal experiences. Indeed, his conclusion may be regarded as a Wilsonian's comment on the Age of Hoover.

"The consequence of all this is apparent," he says. "We see great and cultured cities captured by demagogues; Mayors and even Governors convicted of corruption in office; great public questions discussed in passion and decided on prejudice, while individual and educated men look on in sorrow——but educated men and women as a class are not drawn together and fail to act.

"Meanwhile, in every reasonable public office in the country sits some lonely public servant bearing his burdens without the comforting consciousness, which he is entitled to have, that if he acts uprightly and as wisely as he can, he will be sustained against unjust criticism or interested obstruction, by the concerted action of good and wise men everywhere."

In the fall of 1918 he ventured upon prophecy,

NEWTON D. BAKER

and again this disciple of Saint Woodrow predicted precisely what has befallen a people who deserted Wilsonian ideals to worship at the feet of a Baker-Wilson associate—Herbert Hoover.

"Has all this mechanical development of recent years really advanced us?" he asked. "Has this great civilization of ours, built upon machinery, really meant our refinement? . . . Indeed, is it not possible that we shall see, after the war, that machinery was not our servant, but that we were its slaves?"

These are troublous and unwonted thoughts for a candidate for the presidency. They reveal, clearly, that Mr. Baker is no ordinary fellow, no traditional type of office-seeker. So does his denunciation of the dry laws—which has all the greater merit because he made it as a member of the Wickersham Commission.

Should he ask such questions on the stump—and he will, if nominated—he may awe and affright the people. They will not understand him, perhaps, and they will wonder why, unlike lesser men, he does not prate of such sacred issues as party, prosperity, patriotism.

Will not the voters say of this surprising stranger in their midst what the inhabitants of

THE MIRRORS OF 1932

Martinsburg, West Va., his birthplace, said upon his return from Johns Hopkins University and Washington and Lee Law School? Back home again, young Baker spent his days in a rural law office, his late afternoons in the library, his early evenings in writing reports for his father, who was the local health officer.

Nights he climbed to his attic study, and there, beneath the one electric light in the town, he buried himself, as he still does, in his books. One night a week he gave to German, one to Italian, one to Greek, one to Spanish, one to French and one to British authors.

Eager to become an orator, he often declaimed in tones which, for all their restraint and modulation, carried a strange message across the roofs and spires of the sleeping village. Whereupon the unimpressed natives would say:

"There's Doc Baker's son again. The doc sent him to college and see what a damn fool he's made of him."

GIFFORD PINCHOT

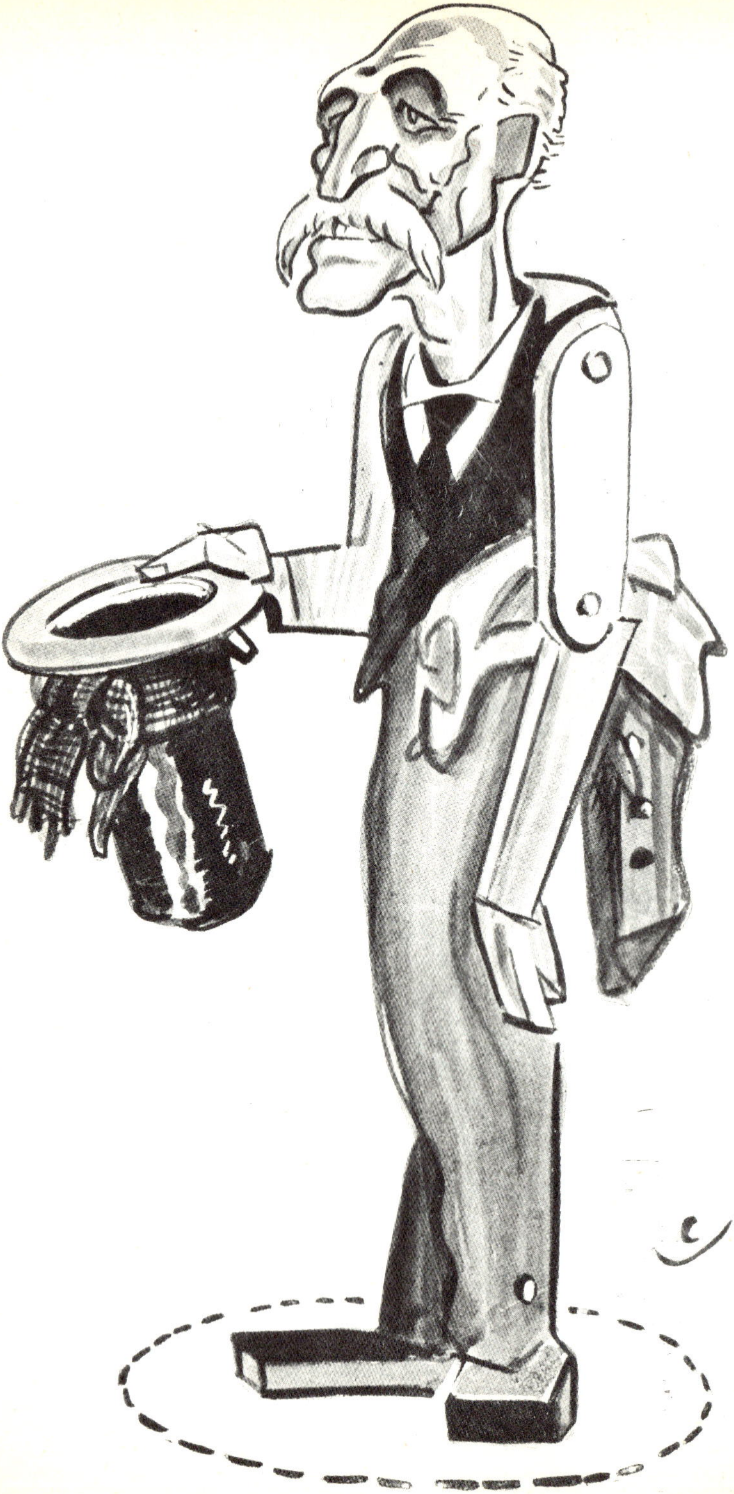

GIFFORD PINCHOT

"Savonarola on a soapbox"—

This characterization, which was originally applied to William E. Borah by Sir Wilmott Lewis, describes Gifford Pinchot even more aptly.

He does not even own the soapbox. It was constructed by the late Theodore Roosevelt, who first put grandiose ideas into the gentle Gifford's head, and the latter has not driven a new nail into it in twenty years.

He has forgotten nothing and learned little. He will pass out, politically, as he has lived—clutching a battered Rooseveltian hat and appealing for the nomination of a Rooseveltian Progressive—himself.

He will be faithful to his last, lonely candidacy—the last of the Roosevelt boys.

No man in American politics has had so many good issues and handled them so ineptly. Even when he was on the right side, he showed an amazing ability for getting himself in wrong. He has been too intense and indiscreet. He has alienated friends and sympathizers drawn to him by the things he has championed.

Men like Mr. Pinchot, though well-intentioned and independent, are largely responsible for the low state of the Progressive cause in this country. He personifies, in the public mind, the erratic and irresponsible nature of our political rebels. They are too intolerant, too intemperate, too grim and too unyielding. Fate, through some strange whim, has endowed the Jim Watsons and the Warren Hardings with the breeziness and bonhomie which, equally with high principles, win men and votes.

Mr. Pinchot is the victim of his enthusiasms. He has espoused too many strange causes. He has been too virulent in his criticism of other men and their motives. He has provoked too many needless disputes within and without his party. There is no restraint in him. He is, in his own view, too righteous. The ordinary man cannot understand such a fellow, and therefore holds him suspect.

There is some justification for suspecting his sincerity in recent years.

He has kept his ear too close to the ground in his

GIFFORD PINCHOT

hunt for issues which he could capitalize. He has taken up too many causes and abandoned too many. He has, when expedient, compromised and trimmed. He has been at all times a supreme showman, sometimes sincere, but always unstable.

Ambition has spoiled him. Had he eschewed politics and been content to rest his fame upon his reputation as a practical conservationist, he would have a definite place in history. His great causes —the rivers, the forest, the power they provide— would have benefited so much the more. But, characteristically, he succumbed to the desire for acclaim and publicity, and he has soiled himself and his principles.

He has permitted his causes to become causeways. He has shown himself more concerned with the devices than with the destiny of democracy.

For a score of years the G.O.P. has deceived or bulldozed him, yet he never toys with the thought of quitting the party. He will not walk out or be kicked out. Like so many other Progressives, he is irregular only between elections and never at campaign time.

Thus he has supported such boisterous Bull Moosers as Charles Evans Hughes, Warren G.

THE MIRRORS OF 1932

Harding, Calvin Coolidge and Herbert Hoover. He denounces them before the conventions are held, indorses them before Election Day, and returns to the attack after they take office.

He has been elected Governor of Pennsylvania twice through the support of the most reactionary figure in semi-public life—Joe Grundy, the high-tariff lobbyist—the intolerant church people of the rural regions and the ladies who sing that "Lips which touch liquor shall never touch mine."

Like Old Bob La Follette, he has been well hazed. The conservatives of his party have propagandized against him since he split the party in 1912. They have labored to create the impression that he is untrustworthy, undependable, the Pierrot of politics. He has been isolated and quarantined as if he were a political leper.

The same traits which have hurt him in politics equipped him to be the apostle of the gospel of conservation. That task required a man of his imagination, his intemperance, his fearlessness. Even his flair for sensationalism and headlines was an asset. That he was an aristocratic millionaire who preferred the woods to yachting, automobiling and society lent a dramatic touch.

It was he who furnished the inspiration and intelligence for Roosevelt's conservation program. He aroused Teddy's slumbering interest in the problem of the forests, the streams, the natural resources. He can explain such problems in language a grammar school child understands and enjoys. He has a personality which wins the respect of men who devote their lives to the woods. It is his happiest and most attractive side.

As soon as he entered politics, however, he entered a decline. More important, he dragged his demi-god, Roosevelt, down with him. In retrospect, it is clear that Mr. Pinchot must bear as great a responsibility as Teddy for precipitating the party split of 1912. Through the lack of restraint he exhibited then, and has ever since, he deeply affected the course of history, and he is an important figure if only for that reason.

The story of the Taft-Roosevelt break is largely the story of Gifford Pinchot. The personal and political disagreement between the two presidential friends may have been inevitable, but there is evidence that Mr. Pinchot, more than any other individual, was responsible. It is little wonder that thoughtful Republicans distrust him.

An impartial review of the Ballinger-Pinchot controversy at this distant day reveals that the forester, as so often happens, acted precipitately and thoughtlessly, though, no doubt, from motives of the best. Mr. Taft had, when Mr. Pinchot entered the picture publicly exonerated Ballinger of the charge that the latter was turning over valuable Alaskan coal lands to the Guggenheims, and a Congressional committee was preparing to investigate the whole question.

Although Mr. Pinchot may have been sincere in his belief that Mr. Taft and Mr. Ballinger were mistaken, it was clear then as it is now that technicalities of the law rather than Roosevelt's central policy of conservation had been forgotten or neglected by the Taft-Ballinger group.

When articles tending to discredit the President began to appear in the magazines as the handiwork of Pinchot's subordinates, Taft's only course was to dismiss the author, one Glavis. When Mr. Pinchot, in a letter that was read on the Senate floor by Senator Dolliver, eulogized Glavis, and also cast doubt on the President's position, he was, clearly, guilty of inexcusable insubordination. The "last of the Roosevelts," by his own deliberate act, made it impossible for Mr. Taft to retain him in office.

Even before his dismissal, however, the "tree

doctor" was making trouble. While still a subordinate of President Taft, he wrote a lengthy epistle to Mr. Roosevelt, who was then in the African jungle, in which he submitted evidence of Taft's betrayal of his predecessor's policies. Some of the reasons outlined by Mr. Pinchot were puerile, some laughable, some pertinent, some impertinent. It may be imagined, however, how this letter that greeted Roosevelt at Khartoum inflamed the latter's suspicious and ambitious spirit.

But—and this is historically important—Mr. Pinchot's hasty action drove Roosevelt to thoughts of rebellion, and Taft into the camp of Republican reactionaries, at the very moment when the President was translating some of the principal Roosevelt policies into legislative reality. Even as Mr. Pinchot was setting the scene for Armageddon, Mr. Taft was framing a conservation and trust-busting program quite as far-reaching as Teddy could wish. He had, likewise, declined to side with "Uncle Joe" Cannon's Old Guard in the battle between House reactionaries and the Norris Progressives.

Mr. Taft, a weak, jovial, judicial figure, was making a supreme effort to be loyal and faithful to the trust which Roosevelt had reposed in him. He was then standing at the crossroads—this was early in his Administration—and it was still doubtful which path he would choose. An evil fate, in the person of Mr. Pinchot, gave the shove which sent him reeling into the arms of the Cannons, the Paynes and the Aldriches.

Although this is, without a doubt, the blackest spot on the Pinchot 'scutcheon, there are many other blotches. Mr. Pinchot undoubtedly acted with a high regard for the public interest, which, as always, he identified with his own, but a wiser course of action would have strengthened his cause. There might have been less drama and smaller headlines—which he would have regretted—but there would have been more sense and fairness in a contrary course.

The incident is typical of Mr. Pinchot and his career. He is always too quick on the trigger, even though the target may deserve his attack.

A simple recital of his ups and downs since the Taft Administration presents a perfect picture of the man. Shallow and superficial, there are no depths to plumb. There is no better way of describing him than to set forth what he has done and said—and how!

For many years after his dismissal by Mr. Taft he dropped out of sight, except for periodical preachments on conservation and warnings to the G.O.P. that it was heading for damnation. In 1922, however, he turned up as Chief Forester under Gov. William Sproul of Pennsylvania. Again he was an opportunist and a mischief-maker.

Upon the death of the late Boies Penrose, Mr. Sproul initiated a movement to unify the Republican leaders behind a single candidate for Governor. But he could not unify Mr. Pinchot. The latter saw his opportunity and he took it.

Prohibition was then the Eleventh Commandment, and, always a personal dry, he made that his principal political issue. He assailed the Pittsburgh and Philadelphia bosses, promising political purity and reduced taxes. Luck was with him, and against a disorganized array of petty bosses he won the primary and the election.

This accomplishment was quite remarkable in view of the numerous comical disputes in which he had engaged during his years of retirement. As a member of Herbert Hoover's relief organization in Belgium he was expelled from the regions controlled by the Germans because, so Mr. Pinchot explained, his sister was married to an Englishman. In the early period of the war he showed characteristic impatience and indiscretion. Hardly a day passed that he did not condemn Woodrow Wilson for not entering the conflict on the side of the Allies.

In 1917 he resigned from Mr. Hoover's Food Administration with a series of denunciations of the future President. Mr. Hoover, he said, was "not a real Republican or a real American," he was "more autocratic than Mr. Wilson." The Food Administrator's sympathies, according to Mr. Pinchot, rested not with the producer or consumer but "with the great special interests—the packers, the canners and the millers."

It is difficult to discover the real reason for Mr. Pinchot's resignation. He was, however, especially wrought up at Mr. Hoover's refusal to guarantee a price for the production of pork. While the fate of peoples hung in the balance, he became excited and patriotic over the price of pigs.

As Governor, he was a happy playboy; he was in his element. He cut his own salary, threw open his office door to all comers, named a woman to high post, invited all state employees at Harrisburg to a dance, forced state officials to sign a prohibition pledge. Again and again he summoned the forty-seven Governors into conference to solve the problems of the nation—by talk and resolutions.

He was shriekingly sensational, but he got the headlines he craves. To suggest an idea was to formulate a new state policy, provided it promised a "good story."

He permitted his indiscretions, his enthusiasms, his imagination, his delusions of grandeur, to run riot. He made the nation's business his affair, and he interfered regularly with the problems of other states. He was, as Sydney Smith said of Daniel Webster, "a steam-engine in trousers," even though he ran without tracks or schedules.

Few fellow-Governors took him seriously. He got a sharp answer from Al Smith when he suggested that New York abandon its suit to have the Federal Water Power Act declared invalid. The Chief Executives of Connecticut and Wisconsin rebuked him when he called a conference to discuss coal problems, urging him to clean up unbearable conditions within his own state. Even "Charlie" Bryan, the Nebraska Progressive, held aloof.

He took up prohibition in a big way. He stripped the uniforms from the state police and transformed them into snoopers. He got an enforcement act but no appropriation from an unsympathetic Legislature, and then begged and obtained $250,000 from the W. C. T. U. So devoted was he to the crusade that William Jennings Bryan offered to swap him for Al Smith.

Elated, he turned his guns on prohibition enforcement by Calvin Coolidge and Andrew W. Mellon. He charged that Mr. Mellon had owned whiskey when the dry laws were enacted, but he could not persuade his good friends, the Methodists, to publish his address. Henry J. Allen, then Governor of Kansas, silenced him for a while with the suggestion that he quit plagiarizing Carrie Nation until he had got rid of the thousands of bar-rooms and speakeasies in Pennsylvania.

Nevertheless, Gifford had a great time. No rebuff bowed him down for long. He is, even more than Al Smith, a "Happy Warrior."

Although he toyed with the idea of entering the presidential primary in 1924, he declined to support that most excellent peanut-and-lemon Progressive, Hiram Johnson of California. He sought election as delegate-at-large to the Republican convention, but he was badly defeated. Nevertheless, he ended up by indorsing Mr. Coolidge.

He bobbed up in the Coolidge inaugural parade astride a great white charger. He wore for picturesque headgear a great black, ten-gallon hat, the gift of Pat Neff of Texas. Smiling and bowing,

GIFFORD PINCHOT

Gifford white-winged Pennsylvania Avenue with his headpiece as he paid obeisance to Mr. Coolidge in front of the White House, but the President was looking in another direction at the moment.

Despite his early differences with Mr. Hoover, Mr. Pinchot supported the Republican candidate in 1928, thus revealing how threadbare his mental and political processes can be upon occasions. Mr. Smith, in his opinion, was right on the two great questions of power and agricultural relief, but Mr. Hoover's strong and sincere (sic) stand on prohibition was the determining factor.

Nevertheless, his offer to take the stump for Mr. Hoover was rejected, and he sat in his tent—no doubt a great hardship to this friend of headlines.

In 1930 he presented himself to the electorate again, and again he struck at the opportune moment. A division over personalities and prohibition within the Pennsylvania organization, together with Grundy's desire for reprisal against the Vare-Mellon alliance, enabled the adventurer to win. In his second term Mr. Pinchot has quite forgotten the idealism which, in words if not in deeds, had hitherto animated him.

Whereas efficiency had been the test of appointments in his first term, expediency now guides him. He employs the methods of the hated machine politicians to build up a personal organization. Forgetting his own disloyalty to Taft, he threatens to dismiss those who decline to support his policies. He quarrels with a Legislature willing to compromise on his latest and greatest issue—more drastic regulation of public utilities.

He exhibits little of the diplomatic ability with which so many Chief Executives wrest favorable action on their proposals from hostile legislative bodies. He prefers to preserve an issue rather than settle it. His second administration, even more than the first, has been barren of accomplishment.

Savonarola adds no cubits to his stature, and there are yet no new nails in the soapbox.

Mr. Pinchot is more attractive as a personality than as a politician. With all his shortcomings, it is to the credit of any man that he shows a definite preference for public service to the leisure which his millions can afford him.

Although he is an eccentric, his personal idiosyncrasies are more picturesque, and less capable of mischief-making, than his political vagaries.

He advertises his democracy. He is an excellent scholar, but he issues statements to the press which are almost as ungrammatical as Mr. Hoover's. He owns several expensive, foreign automobiles, but he campaigns and attends public functions in cars of cheap American manufacture that are always the worse for wear.

He wears the finest of suits, but the story is that he conceals their cut and texture by rumpling them before he puts them on. He never goes abroad without his battered brown hat, brown brogans of coarse grain and soft-collared shirts. His costume rarely varies; he wears the same dress to a fishing expedition that he does to an inaugural ball. Always he looks like a millionaire hobo.

He has the physique of an athlete; he is tall, lanky, lithe, nervous in all his movements. He can hit a woodchuck at 100 yards, but he will not kill small game. It's bears—or elephants—or nothing for Gifford, in the woods and in politics.

Fishing is his favorite sport, and he is as skilled at casting for trout in Pike County, Pa., or in fighting the tarpon off Catalina Island. He owns eight miles of running brooks which are closely guarded by an armed watchman—a peculiarity quite unexplainable in so vocal an advocate of popular sovereignty.

Few men of half his age—he is sixty-five—have

such a superfluity of vitality. In the forests or on the stump he wears out his companions. If a storm comes on while he is fishing or hunting, he simply sits under a tree and sings to himself. If blizzards sweep across the state while he is campaigning, he refuses to shift to a closed car; he pulls a fur coat about him and bares his nearly bald head to the blasts.

He likes the outdoors. If possible, he delivers his speeches at open-air meetings—from the rear of his car, from the tail-end of a truck, from the stoop of a rural store. He delivers a score of speeches a day and shows no fatigue. He has great recuperative powers, physically, and, as his career has shown, spiritually. Perhaps because he has learned the art of sleeping. He can drop off into a sound sleep any time, any place, even if it is for no more than fifteen minutes.

He guards his health like a college athlete. He neither drinks nor smokes, and he watches his food like a dietician. His only luxury in the eating line is hard candy, which he consumes in five-pound lots. He is as intemperate in this respect as some men are with hard liquor. Against the advice of physicians he celebrates victories with sweets which sell for thirty cents a can.

GIFFORD PINCHOT

He has a likable personality; he is affable and approachable. He actually enjoys his contacts with workingmen, farmers, newspaper correspondents, rural politicians.

Although he strives to create the impression that he knows nothing of practical politics, and cares less, he is a consummate vote-getter. He knows all the tricks of the game.

"My name's Pinchot, what's yours?" is his invariable greeting to groups huddled about the general store when his cavalcade sweeps into a rural hamlet.

If this cheery and democratic greeting does not win them immediately, it does not feaze him. He climbs to the store porch, and addresses them in their own idioms. Poking a lean forefinger at them, he discusses the local prices of meat, farm products, electric power, county taxes, market conditions, and even more familiar problems.

These tidbits of local gossip he has been careful to obtain by sending out advance men to collect information for his speeches. Thus he plays upon local prejudices and denounces far-away bosses in Pittsburgh and Philadelphia and Harrisburg —the Mellons, the Vares, the Atterburys, the Cunninghams. Like any vaudeville headliner, he employs all the political gags, grudges and gaucheries.

These soapbox stunts have twice made him Governor of the great Commonwealth of Pennsylvania.

What next—Savonarola?

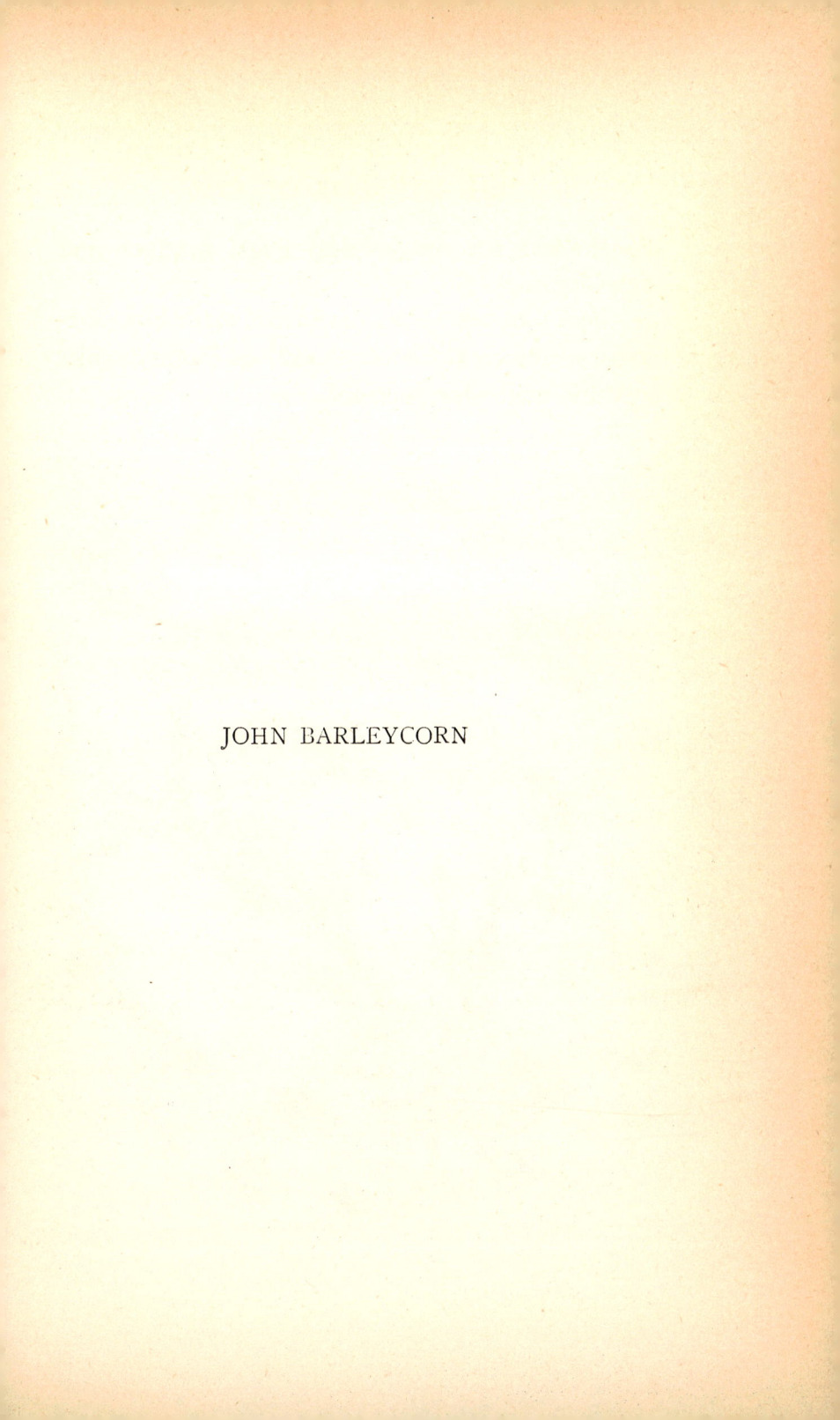

JOHN BARLEYCORN

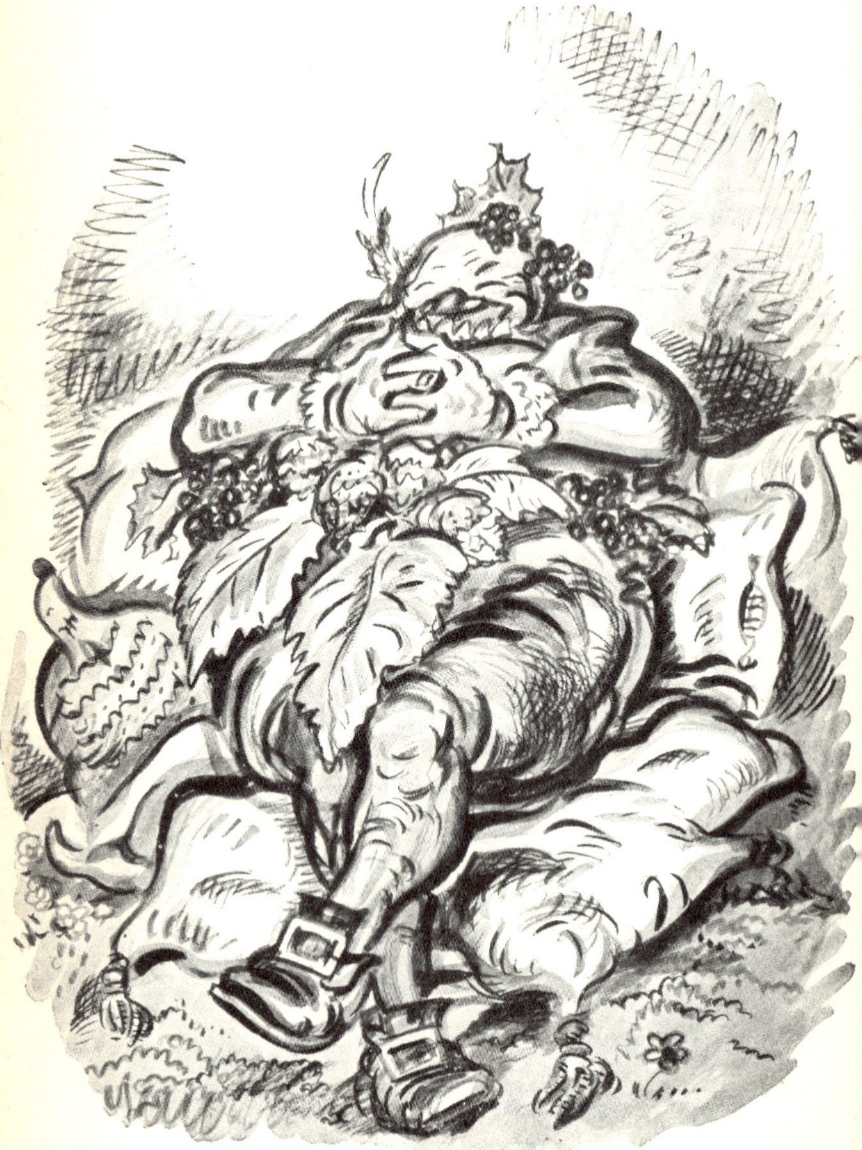

JOHN BARLEYCORN

John Barleycorn, although no presidential candidate, will be the boon companion of presidential candidates in the 1932 campaign.

His spirit, once so gentle and uplifting, will cast a shadow athwart the political scene and the political scene-shifters.

It will burden the hearts and muddy the minds of the two nominees eventually selected to associate with this sober shade.

Platforms may not mention him. Prohibitionists may exorcise him. Politicians may pass him by. Some wets may dodge into a speakeasy to escape him.

Prospective occupants of the White House, with a few exceptions, may not acknowledge his presence. Even those who believe that, as an unburied wraith, he should be given honest burial or lawful resurrection, will not hearken to him.

He will be an issue without a party.

THE MIRRORS OF 1932

Nevertheless, he will dominate American politics even more completely than he has during the dark and drunken decade of 1921–1931.

No matter who the next President will be, he will be the choice of a convention which discharged its solemn and historic duty to the popping of corks, the tinkling of cocktail shakers and the swish-swish of set-ups.

A majority of the delegates, if hilariousness repeats, will spend their time with Old John in speakeasies, friendly lodge halls, civic bars, hotel rooms and a prolonged stupor while they wait upon the decisions of the party bosses and presidential spokesmen. The promptest bootlegger will be a more popular figure than the President or near-President they are about to name.

Federal agents and local police, for the moment, will have important missions elsewhere. The delegates must not be harassed as they ballot and booze. There must be no stupid seizures of artificial and alcoholic aids to a dishonest Democracy as it seeks inspiration—and hangovers.

The nominators, with ballots and booze, will pay honorable if hilarious tribute to the "experiment noble in motive" and to the maker of that wondrous word-puzzle. The author of that masterpiece of statesmanlike slipperiness will be the recipient of many an alcoholic accolade. The delegates, no doubt, will know what he meant.

All will be done and drunk in a spirit of good, clean fun—and in surprisingly good liquor.

Thus America's political hosts—and hostesses—will march unsteadily to the presidential and prohibition wars.

Thus government of the fanciful, by the fanatics and for the feeble-minded will preserve its latter-day nobility. . . .

This is no imaginary description of the circumstances under which Chief Executives are nominated in prohibition America. If anything, it is an understatement. It applies to Republicans and Democrats, wets and drys.

Eloquent pleaders for prohibition will deliver their periods with mints in their mouths and stimulants in their stomachs. Members of platform committees will frame prohibition planks with wavering fingers. And an intoxicating roar from the convention floor will approve these acts.

Nor can this properly be described as sham. It is simply the American system.

If it depicts the hypocrisy of our statesmen, it also delineates the complacency of Presidents and the stupidity of prohibitionists.

Every convention in the Volsteadian era has been

a bacchanalian orgy. Perhaps the wettest and the wobbliest was the Kansas City assemblage which gave us Herbert Hoover. The liquor was excellent, prices were low, service was prompt, the cops were considerate. For those who had not the price there were establishments where drinks were served free by broad-minded boosters of the municipality.

Whether he knows it or not, Mr. Hoover's presidential bark was launched upon a sea of liquor—good liquor, too, he may be glad to learn.

Although the Houston convention which nominated Al Smith was no Anti-Saloon League meeting, it was an orderly and sober affair by comparison with that holy consecration of the Grand Old Party to the things of the spirit. Old John Barleycorn, verily, was as much of a headliner there as were Honorable William E. Borah, Mabel Walker Willebrandt—and Mr. Hoover.

Nor is it only to the threshold of the White House that our politicians tote their flasks. They carry these alcoholic appurtenances of modern America to the edge of the grave itself.

In making Presidents and in burying their honored dead they do it with drinking. . . .

Present at the funeral of a Republican chieftain

so distinguished that, but for his death, his name would have been included in this gallery of half-gods, was the customary delegation of honorary pallbearers chosen by the Congress of the United States. In this instance the riotous goings-on of most Congressional funeral parties were temporarily stilled and repressed.

The official pallbearers, with sad, shiny eyes and black, shiny suits, behaved most decorously—that is, for Congressional junkets. They got generous mileage and headlines as they sped toward the city which was the place of burial. They shared publicity with a President and many members of the Cabinet. They departed from the cemetery with bowed heads and subdued hearts. A great and gay comrade had gone the way of all flesh.

Some left immediately for home, some for the Capital. One merry group, however, spent the afternoon and evening in a comfortable brewery no great distance from the graveyard.

Amidst the vats and kegs they danced and drank and sang and made whoopee. It was such a scene as Hogarth might have yearned to paint. Far into the night they celebrated with a conviviality which vanished only as the beer ran low.

One gargantuan fellow, worn out from clumsy

demonstrations of how to win votes by dancing bridal polkas at backwoods weddings in the Northwest, sank into a heavy slumber. His snores resounded like thunder through the barnlike brewery.

A realistic picture of prohibition in repose, to his associates he presented an excellent opportunity for non-partisan fun. He awoke to a scurrying and squealing which were but the blithesome noises of our statesmen at play.

As he clambered to his feet, a familiar odor stirred his nostrils. Slowly his senses returned to him, and through the smell of stale beer he detected the acrid fumes of limburger cheese. Brushing his eyes, he discovered that his inebriate and exuberant fellows had splashed his trouser legs with a thick, yellow layer of limburger. In his pockets, for good measure, they had stuck kippered herrings—the remains of their supper.

A crude and unlovely picture, perhaps.

Nevertheless, it is one which, with the convention canvass, reflects the spirit of hypocrisy that animates the men who make our laws and our Presidents. The two scenes present a panorama of prohibition which cannot be matched in all the volumes of a Wickersham Report.

Mr. Hoover, without a doubt, knows that these conditions exist. To argue otherwise is to imply an obtuseness or a deliberate disregard of realities even he is not guilty of.

Attorney General Mitchell, the Prohibition Poohbah, likewise is aware of the persistence of these peccadilloes, although he is so constituted that he can be ignorant, legally and officially, of more things than any other man in high office.

His prohibition assistants—Aaron Youngquist and Amos W. W. Woodcock—may or may not know what is going on about them, above them, below them. It does not matter. They are mere figureheads. Mr. Youngquist, a dour Scandinavian, dare not open his lips to tell the time of day, Mr. Woodcock opens his too often.

Withal, the wets should be thankful that Mr. Hoover was elected rather than Mr. Smith. Whereas the latter might have leaned backwards in an effort to refute Hooverish charges that he was a nullificationist, Mr. Hoover, in the guise of a friend, outwits and deceives the prohibitionists.

Every day in every way he seeks to ease the discontent of the wets without losing the affection of the drys. He hands hymns to the drys and highballs to the wets.

So far he has succeeded remarkably well.

Slowly but surely the Hoover Administration whittles away at the Grand Old Law. Through strange interpretations and administration of the statute, it has, by degrees, removed large fields of liquefaction from the jurisdiction of the Eighteenth Amendment and the Volstead Act.

It permits, for instance, the manufacture and sale of a grape concentrate which becomes, through the simple operation of natural laws that are carefully explained by the salesmen, 15 per cent. wine. It sanctions, with legal salvings of its conscience, home brew, and, parenthetically, hard liquor of the kitchen sink variety.

Mr. Woodcock, unlike his predecessors, painstakingly and publicly explains the legal right of every citizen to be his own brewmaster and distiller. He devotes as much energy to instructing his agents in what they cannot do as he does to lecturing them upon their legal prerogatives. He is, if the wets only knew it, a most excellent officer of the law.

These subtle assaults upon the dry laws are not haphazard or unpremeditated. They are a definite manifestation of Mr. Hoover's philosophy. It is only political expediency which prevents him from an aggressive and advertised movement to weaken prohibition's legislative bulwarks.

In his words the President is a prohibitionist, in his works he is our first presidential nullifier.

In his heart he has no more sympathy for compulsory and Congressional prohibition than Al Smith himself.

He is, with respect to this great social and economic problem, only a politician, and not a very courageous one.

He labored for days to frame the ambiguous definition of prohibition that gave cheer to both wets and drys in the Republican Party in 1928. Although he misinterpreted and ignored the Wickersham Commission's recommendation for revision, he secretly informed correspondents for wet, Republican newspapers that this did not mean he was a dry.

If he did not inspire, he did approve the address which former Representative Franklin Fort delivered in favor of virtual exemption of alcoholic beverages made at home for consumption in the home. The President's denial that he held his friend's views, like his characterization of prohibition and his handling of the Wickershammer's Report, was purposely ambiguous.

The White House statement said that Mr. Fort was expressing his own ideas, but it refrained from saying that these were not Mr. Hoover's ideas. And George Akerson, then secretary to Mr. Hoover, winked as he distributed the communique.

There is yet another test. The price of liquor at the Capital and elsewhere has steadily declined since Mr. Hoover entered the White House. The quality continues to improve. The bootleggers in the business buildings which tower above the presidential mansion grow more bold. Indeed, purveyors of liquor are seen more frequently in the corridors of departmental structures and Congress than representatives of the dry organizations.

Such is the present state of prohibition in America.

Mr. Hoover seeks to lay the ghost of John Barleycorn without benefit of Congress or the courts.

Moreover, the President has made the professional prohibitionists like it.

The change which has come over the anointed apostles of aridity is reflected in the chameleonlike conduct of Mrs. Willebrandt. Once a coworker

JOHN BARLEYCORN

with the Anti-Saloon League and the Methodist Board, a pulpit-ranter for Mr. Hoover in 1928, she now emerges as the super-lawyer for the grape concentrate interests.

The Carrie Nation of the drys has become the Clara Barton of the wets. She is engaged in applying vinous liquid to heal the wounds she gave in 1928. It is the most remarkable transformation in all the ten years of prohibition, as she is the most challenging figure of the dry decade.

She is the smart little heroine of this California comedy. Herself a Californian, she has wrung a blessing and a legalization from a California President for the wine of California grapes. From another Californian—C. C. Teague, late of the Federal Farm Board—she obtained federal funds with which to finance the grape concentrate industry.

A smart girl is Mabel. As Assistant Attorney General in charge of liquor prosecutions, she got decisions from the Supreme Court which were designed to make America actually bone-dry. In fact, one outlawed the sale of appliances for the home-manufacture of liquor—kegs, copper coils, bottle cappers, malt and hops. She was then the darling of the drys, and they envisaged the happy day when even nature's anti-prohibition processes might be rendered null and void.

Then all her song was "Take to your pulpits, ye parsons." Now it is "Take to your cellars, ye wets."

As lawyer and lobbyist for the grape-makers, she has been quite as artful as when she stumped the Bible Belt for Mr. Hoover. She got the grant of federal funds with the argument that grapes shipped in liquid form would keep them out of the hands of Al Capone, and thereby lessen the resources of bootleggers and gangsters of the underworld.

She has, in short, hallowed her employers' product.

More important still for the light it casts upon the little lady, she has won the drys to grudging approval of this program. As she incited them to riot against Al Smith in 1928, so she has kept them from denouncing herself and Mr. Hoover for the breach they have made in the law. She has disproved the adage that a man—or woman—cannot serve two masters—or three in a prohibition pinch.

It is true that for a while the guardians of abdominal morality gazed upon this studied weakening of the dry laws with suspicion. It seemed to them that their prohibitory paradise was growing more mundane and less moral through no apple but a grape, through no Eve but a Mabel.

The prospect once brought denunciations from the ordained spokesmen for the drys—the Cannons, the McBrides, the Wilsons. Soon, however, they were made to see the light. Presidential emissaries let them know that, albeit Mr. Hoover might take away the substance of the law, he would not deprive them of the law itself.

So long as he gets the votes, they may have the statutes—an arrangement eminently satisfactory to these godly men.

With this they must rest content. Now all their talk is of checking the traffic rather than the appetite—a complete abdication of their original purpose. They profess to be quite satisfied with Mr. Hoover's policies.

Hoist with their own President, they have no alternative.

Should the Democratic Party become lawless and liquid, as may happen, the drys must remain with the Republican Party even though it be dry in name only. Otherwise, they will have no place to go. They might conceivably have to go out of business. There would then be no more collections, no more fat salaries, no more opportunities for the satisfaction of their sadistic impulses.

Strange as it may seem, the professional prohibitionists now prefer Mr. Hoover to any other candidate, with the possible exception of Calvin Coolidge or Gifford Pinchot. Weak Presidents are their stock in trade, and Mr. Hoover is weak; he may undermine the law but he will never publicly profane it.

Governor Pinchot, as President, would redramatize the cause and boost collections, and what true prohibitionist can ask more! Calvin's lackadaisical nature, however, has a special appeal for the drys, even though he once eliminated from a state document a eulogy of prohibition inadvertently inserted by his ghost writer. He permitted the moralizers to dictate policies and patronage, and his latchstring was always out to Anti-Saloon League runners.

Franklin D. Roosevelt has declared for repeal, to be sure, but he inspires little fear or hatred among the drys. They suspect that, once in the White House, he will make no move to endanger the dry laws. They believe that his history and background incline him to little more than political sympathy with the wets.

JOHN BARLEYCORN

Toward Joe Robinson, Owen D. Young and Albert C. Ritchie the drys are quite indifferent, largely because they discount the chances of all three for the nomination.

Three men they fear—Al Smith, Newton D. Baker and Dwight W. Morrow.

Honest and forthright men they cannot abide. They know, too, that these three, as candidates or nominees—and especially Mr. Smith or Mr. Baker —would invite, indeed welcome, John Barleycorn to the political festivities.

However—invited or omitted, wanted or unwanted, guest or ghost—this spectral Old Soak will make—and break—Presidents and parties.